TRUE TO ONE ANOTHER

'Arnold is a gateway poet whose poetry helps us better appreciate the poetic world before him, as well as appreciate the turns that poetry took after him; he also happens to be a hugely enjoyable read!'

DALJIT NAGRA
Author of *Look We Have Coming to Dover!*

'Sylvia Plath recalled loving Arnold's *The Forsaken Merman*, which her mother would read to her. Arnold offers readers resonant connection to the depth and mystery of our lives; he has continued significance for present-day poets and readers. Certainly, for me, he has been a poet-companion along my own path since my teens and continues so today.'

PENELOPE SHUTTLE
Author of *Redgrove's Wife*

True to One Another

POEMS BY
MATTHEW ARNOLD

SELECTED BY
JOHN GREENING
WITH AN INTRODUCTION AND NOTES

RENARD PRESS

RENARD PRESS LTD

124 City Road
London EC1V 2NX
United Kingdom
info@renardpress.com
020 8050 2928

www.renardpress.com

The poems in this volume first published 1849–69
This selection first published by Renard Press Ltd in 2025

Edited text, notes, introduction and selection © John Greening, 2025
'Further Stanzas from the Grande Chartreuse' © John Greening, 2025.
First published in *The Interpretation of Owls: Selected Poems 1977–2022*,
ed. Kevin Gardner (Texas: Baylor University Press, 2023).
Reprinted by kind permission of Baylor University Press.
'A Walk with Matthew Arnold' © John Greening, 2025

Cover design by Will Dady

Printed and bound in the UK on carbon-balanced papers by CMP Books

ISBN: 978-1-80447-144-9

9 8 7 6 5 4 3 2 1

CLIMATE POSITIVE Renard Press is proud to be a climate positive publisher, removing more carbon from the air than we emit and planting a small forest. For more information see renardpress.com/eco.

All rights reserved. This publication may not be reproduced, stored in a retrieval system or transmitted, in any form or by any means – electronic, mechanical, photocopying, recording or otherwise – without the prior permission of the publisher.

EU Authorised Representative: Easy Access System Europe – Mustamäe tee 50, 10621 Tallinn, Estonia, gpsr.requests@easproject.com.

CONTENTS

Introduction	7
True to One Another	
Mycerinus	27
A Question	32
Shakespeare	33
In Utrumque Paratus	34
from Resignation	36
The Forsaken Merman	42
To a Republican Friend, 1848	47
Quiet Work	48
Switzerland	49
MEETING	49
PARTING	50
ISOLATION. TO MARGUERITE	54
TO MARGUERITE — CONTINUED	56
A FAREWELL	57
ABSENCE	61
The Terrace at Berne	62
from Stanzas in Memory of the Author of *Obermann*	65
Youth's Agitations	68
from Empedocles on Etna	69
from Tristram and Iseult	73
Faded Leaves	75
THE RIVER	75
TOO LATE	77
SEPARATION	78
ON THE RHINE	75
LONGING	80

Memorial Verses	81
The Youth of Nature	84
Dover Beach	89
The Buried Life	91
Lines Written in Kensington Gardens	95
The Future	97
A Summer Night	101
Stanzas from the Grande Chartreuse	105
Sohrab and Rustum	113
The Scholar-Gipsy	142
Requiescat	151
from Balder Dead	152
Haworth Churchyard	153
Rugby Chapel	158
Stanzas from Carnac	166
Rachel	168
West London	170
Worldly Place	171
Thyrsis	172
Palladium	181
A Wish	182
Growing Old	185
'Below the surface-stream'	187
The Last Word	188
Note on the Text	189
Notes on the Poems	190
Recommended Reading	197
Acknowledgments	198
Index of Titles	199
Appendix: Two Poems by John Greening	200

INTRODUCTION

Waiting for the Spark from Heaven

Sometimes in appreciating a work of art you have to stick to your guns. How many music lovers wondered what was wrong with them when they read in a standard music guide of the 1950s that Rachmaninov 'made a mark though possibly not a lasting one... inspired by no very strong national or personal feeling'? I must say I have had such moments with the poetry of Matthew Arnold. When I was studying literature, the general view seemed to be that he was a critic of major importance but really (apart perhaps from that glorious anomaly, 'Dover Beach') as a poet he wasn't up to much – too humourless, too intense. Meanwhile, I was enjoying his work rather in the same way I enjoyed Rachmaninov, relishing the intensity, and didn't really know what to do with that enthusiasm. I tempered it, as one does, accepted what I was told – that his friend Arthur Hugh Clough was a much better and more modern poet – and moved on to discover T.S. Eliot.

Eliot in fact wrote an essay on Arnold (see bibliography on p. 198) in which he presented him as an academic figure who offers not much excitement and 'little technical interest', yet he still regarded him as essential reading, unexpectedly 'intimate', a poet to whom he returned with pleasure. While challenging Arnold's own remark that 'poetry is at bottom a criticism of life' and his tendency to confuse poetry and morals, Eliot also found him admirably honest. Not many other poets have written about Arnold's poetry since. What Arnold himself wrote about poetry has had plenty of attention, and it is other critics (such as Lionel Trilling) who have generally been gatekeepers of the work. In the 1990s, Ian Hamilton reminded us of the poet's existence with a short biography and a selection of his verse (minus introduction or notes). But as for today's poetry critics… Occasional enthusiasts show themselves on social media: Lucy Newlyn recently posted 'Memorial Verses', calling it 'one of the greatest elegies ever written', and John Clegg quoted 'Thyrsis' as 'some of the very best poetry in the nineteenth century'. But even Arnold's successors as Oxford Professor of Poetry have for the most part ignored him – though Roy Fuller gave a lecture on that resonant phrase, 'Sweetness and Light'. His son, John Fuller, discusses the little-known poem 'In Utrumque Paratus' in his 2011 book *Who is Ozymandias?*; Carol Rumens analysed 'Dover Beach' (what else?) in her *Guardian* online Poem of the Week in 2008; U.A. Fanthorpe once mentioned the influence on her of 'The Forsaken Merman'; Eavan Boland used to speak of how Arnold helped illuminate her own 'lyric moment'. But he is nowhere to be found in the index of, say, Hughes's or Heaney's or Larkin's letters; few poets allude to him, let alone take him as a benchmark or give him extended attention. As for the shelves of bookshops: you will look in vain between Armitage, Attila the Stockbroker and Auden.

Yet there have been plenty of editions of Matthew Arnold over the past two centuries, and the raw texts are all available unedited online. However, his poems were written for the page, not for the screen, and they are most pleasurably consumed that way. They also benefit from some context and a few background notes. The aim of this new edition is to make reading Arnold a much more satisfying and complete (and portable) experience, and to offer discreet guidance, one poet from the 2020s introducing another from the mid 1800s. Tastes change. The poems we now find moving and relevant are not necessarily those which were important to Arnold's contemporaries – or indeed to his twentieth-century heirs, whose instinct was to tear down what they inherited from the Victorians. Now we are well into a different century and have a better appreciation of that much-maligned period, it seems a good time to reconsider him.

In revisiting his work, I was deeply moved once again by the power of old favourites, especially those that tell a story. 'Sohrab and Rustum' is almost nine hundred lines, but it holds the attention like a film – certain moments with Ruksh, the faithful horse, are pure Hollywood. I've included the entire narrative in this selection. Only the most resilient readers are likely to be dry-eyed by the time they hear that 'longed-for dash of waves' and the waters of the Oxus 'Emerge, and shine upon the Aral Sea'. But I also found several poems I had underestimated when I first read them in the 1970s, poems that oblige us think as well as feel. Some (such as 'The Buried Life') seem to be carrying the torch of Wordsworth the philosopher, and indeed there are two that commemorate him ('Memorial Verses' and 'The Youth of Man'). Several strike me now as much more attuned to our time – the love poems in particular, but also Arnold's metrically relaxed tribute to Harriet Martineau and the Brontës ('Haworth Churchyard') and his late commemoration of the 'bromance' with Clough ('Thyrsis'). His explorations of depression, as we would now call it (and indeed suicide, in 'Empedocles on Etna') might almost foreshadow Alvarez's *The New Poetry*, while the father–son dynamic in 'Sohrab and Rustum' could be from any number of American movies – and even touches on the topical question of stubborn ageing leaders ('if Iran's chiefs are old, then I/Am older'). Readers may also find themselves struck by the relevance of certain outbursts of frustration at 'men's impious uproar'. When in one of his last poems he resignedly snaps that 'Geese are swans, and swans are geese./Let them have it how they will' I can't help imagining someone slamming their laptop shut in disgust at social media. For all its mannerisms, Matthew Arnold's voice can sound very modern indeed, not least when he is in his plain-spoken mode and when he experiments with free verse as he does in 'Rugby Chapel'. Nor are all his poems elegiac, although (as with certain Russian composers) it's when contemplating loss that he's at his most moving. What you will find here are what I consider the most enduring, the most accessible as well as the most representative pieces.

If you are new to Arnold – and I hope some of you are – then can I suggest that for the longer poems you don't skim them as if they were prose. I'd advise finding a quiet place and actually reading them aloud, not worrying about the meaning, but relishing the rhythms, the shifts in metre, the line breaks and the sound. You can find actors performing them online, but it's better to have a go yourself: the very attempt brings you closer to the workings of the machine. When I was a teacher I used to read the entirety of 'The Forsaken Merman' to classes of quite boisterous children, and the poem's extraordinary soundscape invariably held their attention. Disney's *The Little Mermaid* might have worked even better, but Arnold's monodrama is poignant and compelling. 'The Scholar-Gipsy' too is a poem I have read aloud to sixth-formers and older groups. This musical aspect of the work has been strangely overlooked, perhaps because of Eliot's misguided judgement that he had an unreliable ear and lacked 'auditory imagination'. We have heard much of Tennyson's mellifluous music (those 'immemorial elms') and of Browning's speech rhythms ('Zooks!' 'How say I?'), but little is said about Arnold's unique blend of the conversational and the loftily lyrical. The poet capable of 'Dover Beach' and 'To Marguerite' did not suddenly acquire and then lose that gift. It is in most of his work. Yes, there are duds, but fewer than in his great hero Wordsworth.

The name Matthew Arnold meant something to me long before I read him properly, since the day my mother handed me her 1942 school anthology, curiously bound in a soft blue cloth, *Selections from Tennyson, Browning and* (notice how he is always placed last, despite the initial A) *Arnold*. 'The Scholar-Gipsy' was one of my mother's favourite poems, just as 'Sohrab and Rustum' was one of my father's, which is why I have dedicated this new selection to their memory. But the poem I first came to love after 'The Scholar-Gipsy' – whose idyllic lyricism and familiar Thameside settings were beguiling from the start – is 'Stanzas from the Grande Chartreuse', lines that can still move me profoundly. When I discovered this poem, I was in a fairly active religious phase of my life, which was at the time fairly monk-like, so perhaps that's why it struck a chord, although of course Arnold was beset by doubts, and there are passages in his poem that recall Larkin's 'Church Going'. But it's also a poem resulting from a challenging walk, which appealed to me. Some recent stanzas of my own (in the appendix) tell the story behind those of Matthew Arnold.

I suspect for most people their knowledge of Arnold is confined to 'Dover Beach'. If a poet is only to be remembered for a single poem, then this is a magnificent candidate. It's one of those pieces that has taken on a life of its own, lines poached from it to include (or give titles to) films and novels. It is much parodied and pondered by other poets, from Anne Stevenson's 'Dover Beach Reconsidered' to Anthony Hecht's 'The Dover Bitch' and Daljit Nagra's 'Look We Have Coming to Dover!'. It was even set to music by Samuel Barber. What makes it such a success? The place itself helps: there is a universality to the name which was there when Gloucester stood on its cliffs in *King Lear* and was still resonating when Vera Lynn recorded her famous WW2 hit. But more than anything it's the poem's own pulsing music, potent imagery and that sure sense of architecture, how to place a pause or a rhyme, the effortless manner in which line breaks, syntax, alliteration and sibilance evoke the motion of a breaking wave:

> Listen! you hear the grating roar
> Of pebbles which the waves draw back, and fling,
> At their return, up the high strand,
> Begin, and cease, and then again begin,
> With tremulous cadence slow, and bring
> The eternal note of sadness in.

INTRODUCTION

This is an intellectual talking to us, a teacher, but he's won us over so persuasively in the opening 'sonnet' that when he brings up Sophocles we don't feel it's pretentious. Even when he's in danger of preaching and over-stretching an analogy ('The Sea of Faith/Was once, too, at the full…') we are carried swiftly along to meet that miraculous rolling length of onomatopoeia: 'Its melancholy, long, withdrawing roar'. The poem is in a radically free form for the 1850s, with irregular rhyme and stress patterns. He is doing in verse what Turner – who died the year this was composed – was doing on canvas. And what might have been a sentimental ending is genuine feeling, nailed home by the introduction of that unexpected and somehow open-ended epic simile in the final lines, with all its noisy clashing consonants. I hardly think one can accuse this poet of lacking 'auditory imagination'.

Surprisingly enough, Matthew Arnold was a very playful man, but that aspect of his personality rarely comes out in his poetry, which always seems to aspire to some 'high white star', those 'mountain tops where is the throne of Truth'. His family and friends, nonplussed by the high seriousness in his first book, had probably expected something like the Cavalier poets or Edward Lear rather than all these philosophical and elegiac pieces. But there is a twinkle in the poet's eye sometimes when one least expects it – like that straight-faced joke the teacher makes even to an unruly class. The natural world seems to bring out something more genial in him, as when he is reminiscing to his sister in 'Resignation' or in the otherwise bleak 'Empedocles on Etna', when Callicles sings his wood-notes wild. Whenever I find a particular passage in Matthew Arnold that feels too stuffy or self-regarding or merely too distantly Victorian, I remind myself that he held down an irksome day job visiting dreary institutions and dreamed of retiring to sunnier climes, and that all his friends called him Matt. I shall add a short biography here since, whatever T.S. Eliot's views on keeping the life and the work separate, I think it's helpful to know such things.

Born on Christmas Eve, 1822 in Laleham-on-Thames, near Staines, Matthew Arnold was the second of nine children. They were all worked hard at home (Latin at the age of five, Greek by six) and very much under the thumb of their father, Thomas Arnold, Rugby School's celebrated headmaster. After an unhappy period at a boarding school and some private tuition, Matthew was sent to Winchester and then Rugby itself. Young Matt seems to have been something of a disappointment at first – a drifter, too nonchalant, inclined to foppishness, frequently 'droll', though fond of sport – despite misshapen legs, whose condition wasn't much improved by an enforced period in leg irons as a toddler. It gave his father the excuse to nickname him Crab. The boy began writing verse when he was very young, including some lines contemplating 'the murmur of the sea' in a way that anticipates his most famous poem and many others in which moving water is present. Equally important to the developing poet was the mountain scenery of the Lake District, where the family had a house built, which they named Fox How (there was much advice from the Wordsworths, who became good friends). If we are more inclined to associate Arnold's poetry with the tranquil river meadows around Oxford, it's important to think of his many real and imaginary encounters with wilder nature, from the mountains of the Grande Chartreuse to Etna itself. The Arnold family travelled widely and most of them walked enthusiastically.

INTRODUCTION

At Rugby, Matthew was immediately aware of Arthur Hugh Clough, four years his senior. Clough represented everything Dr Arnold wanted to see in his protégés: a model pupil who had won every possible prize. Clough often stayed with the Arnold family (his parents were in America) and there were inevitable comparisons between the boys' respective achievements. It is generally felt that Matthew wasn't too troubled by the disparity and their shared poetic ambitions eventually brought them together. Lord Byron's *Childe Harold's Pilgrimage* was a key influence on young Matthew and his very Byronic poem, 'Alaric at Rome', won the Sixth Form Poetry Prize. It was his first publication, and he even recited the poem with an impressive maturity to the assembled school. It's a remarkable achievement for an eighteen-year-old. When he went on to win a scholarship to Balliol College, Oxford (a city full of anti-Tractarian Arnoldians) his father could not believe it any more than he could believe that Clough had only managed a second-class degree at the same college.

Matthew wisely avoided the kind of theological disputes that broke the spirit of his future friend. He seemed more inclined to prove he was a different beast from his father, especially when Dr Arnold became Professor Arnold and his lectures began to be the talk of the university. Arnold Junior, meanwhile, continued to be jaunty in his manner, dilatory in his studies and stories of his pranks and misdeeds (drinking, gambling, messing around on the Cherwell) began to circulate. His brother Tom's title for this haughty layabout, 'The Emperor' seems quite apt. Nevertheless, it wasn't all nude swimming; there was the Newdigate Prize too, for his poem about Oliver Cromwell.

The sudden death of Thomas Arnold (in his forties) shocked his family, who were already reeling from Jane's broken engagement; the later poem 'Rugby Chapel' conveys something of how persistently the loss affected Matthew, but it's also clear from a poem begun shortly afterwards. The long Egyptian-themed 'Mycerinus' dwells on the idea of premature death; the developing poet had begun to fear he too might die young. He was certainly urging himself on to produce some high-quality poetry, such as the sonnet on Shakespeare. But his university career was not distinguished, and he had to find a way of making a living. He tried teaching at Rugby, but was too much of a rebel, too willing to join in when the boys cheered at a half-day holiday, and some colleagues felt he had too high an opinion of himself. He managed to secure a fellowship at Oriel, and with the help of Goethe, Kant, Descartes, Emerson, Carlyle, began to grow up. Goethe in particular would become one of his guiding lights. The friendship with Clough flourished too, and his letters are full of what sounds like passion ('Oh my love suffer me to stop a little'… 'Oh my love goodnight') although this has been taken more as evidence of what Ian Hamilton calls (in his biography, *A Gift Imprisoned*) 'dandiacal grandeur'. He adds that in early Victorian society 'same-sex intensities and jealousies could flourish publicly without observers assuming that the two friends had gone to bed'. There was no lack of attention to the opposite sex either, especially during his visits to France, where he was in thrall to both George Sand and the actress known simply as 'Rachel' (later commemorated in a group of sonnets). More significantly, during a walking holiday in the Alps, there was a mysterious encounter with a blue-eyed girl who would become the 'Marguerite' of his

Switzerland poems. The woman who was perhaps most important in his life during these years – though hardly in the Dorothy Wordsworth league – was his sister, Jane ('K'), subject of 'Resignation', in which she is 'Fausta'.

A change of government led to a new opportunity for Matthew as Private Secretary to the Whigs' Chancellor of the Exchequer, Lord Lansdowne, at his town house in Fitzmaurice Place, south of Berkeley Square. It proved to be an undemanding job, and conveniently coincided with an upsurge of poetic creativity; but it was Clough – the restless traveller, ablaze with radical fervour – who caught the reading world's attention with his first collection. Arnold was aiming for something loftier than *The Bothie of Toper-Na-Fuosich*, yet didn't want to end up sounding like Tennyson either. His own first book, *The Strayed Reveller and Other Poems*, was published in 1849 under the enigmatic authorship of 'A'. Its seriousness came as a welcome shock to friends and family who had thought of him as incorrigibly flippant. The world-weary scepticism, however, they considered somewhat un-Arnoldian, and his sister (along with some reviewers) felt that he wasn't offering his readers enough comfort or moral guidance.

In an age when, as Keats had suggested, the long poem was considered the 'Polar star of poetry', he already had ideas for 'Empedocles on Etna', but first he headed back to Switzerland, and presumably to blue-eyed Marguerite. Their break-up may have precipitated his stanzas in response to Étienne Pivert de Senancour's prose-poem, *Obermann*, about a trainee priest who flees to the Alps, and perhaps even prompted him to begin 'Tristram and Iseult' (which ended up at some eight hundred lines). The crisis certainly led to the fine lyric Switzerland sequence, with its much-anthologised poems to Marguerite. Arnold was writing fluently and prolifically at this time — there is the distinguished elegy to Wordsworth in 1850, 'Memorial Verses' — but much of what fed into the poems was kept from his family. He was good at compartmentalising. He confided in Clough, but as far as the rest of the world was concerned he was just getting on with his day job at Lansdowne House. Then he met Frances Lucy Wightman.

'Flu', as she was nicknamed, begins to creep in to certain poems from these months (e.g. the 'Faded Leaves' sequence), but Arnold's feelings are seldom straightforward and invariably lead him into more complex areas of morality — as in 'The Buried Life'. Somewhat unfortunately, the Lucy poems tend to merge with the Marguerite poems, although it has been pointed out that when grey eyes are mentioned they must be Lucy's. The relationship had its early difficulties, and her father forbade them to meet, making it clear that Matthew needed a better job if they were to marry. So the young poet applied to be Inspector of Schools (the Old Boys' Network was useful here: the Education Secretary had taught him at Balliol), and the engagement was announced in spring 1851. It still wasn't all plain sailing. He felt ill and anxious as the wedding day approached, and Clough regarded Lucy as his enemy ('Shall I any longer breakfast with Matt twice a week?'). The month-long honeymoon was a veritable Grand Tour, taking them initially to Dover for the cross-channel ferry. It has been speculated that 'Dover Beach' was begun that night, which would have been inconsiderate to say the least; yet Matthew had no qualms about letting his bride take separate accommodation some days later when they visited the male preserve of the Grande Chartreuse. One suspects that he sensed a poem coming on. The resulting stanzas hardly read like the offspring of a honeymoon. Their most memorable lines speak of 'Wandering between two worlds, one dead,/The other powerless to be born'. But Matthew Arnold's wandering was about to be considerably reduced and confined largely to the elementary schools of England.

Arnold must have been all too aware that he was already of advanced age for a lyric poet ('past thirty and three parts iced over') and that he had 'dawdled and scrupled and fiddle-faddled' through his most precious years. Tennyson's new best-seller, *In Memoriam*, can't have helped his mood. But his own writing had to fit in to the arduous new routine of work as an HMI, and very quickly to the arrival of a sickly baby – by the late 1850s, there would be four children – although Lucy was living with her parents while he was travelling. Life for the late Fellow of Oriel was suddenly much less glamorous as he exhausted himself shuttling between cheap lodgings, remote schoolrooms and the home of his in-laws. Yet he took the work seriously and did it thoroughly, becoming Chief Inspector of Schools shortly before his retirement – a title which, alas, brought no extra income. He might drily compare himself to Empedocles, but showed no inclination to despair, although his poems can be relied on to sympathise with anyone imprisoned by 'unmeaning taskwork', and he always had a special respect for poets like Goethe who were in paid employment. He has become (as his biographer Nicholas Murray puts it) 'the patron saint of those who have struggled to do serious intellectual work at the same time as holding down a conventional job'. Arnold consoled himself with trips to Fox How in the school holidays and went on writing as and when he could.

Late in 1852, a gathering of recent work was published by Longman: *Empedocles on Etna and Other Poems* – once again by the anonymous 'A'. Arnold immediately had doubts about the book and insisted that the five hundred copies be withdrawn, offering to replace it with something more varied and less intense, a kind of 'New and Selected'. *Poems (1853)* would even have his full name on the cover and a now-celebrated Preface setting out some of the poet's ideas on his art. Thomas Longman was evidently a very understanding publisher, and it is just as well: the new book was successful and generally well received (though not by Clough). It featured some of Arnold's best work, including some recent narrative work to replace 'Empedocles', which he now considered too morbid and long-winded. One notable addition was 'The Scholar-Gipsy', a magical piece of lyrical filigree spun around a legend of the Thames Valley. But perhaps the most arresting to a modern readership is 'Sohrab and Rustum', Homeric in its aspirations, yet consistently accessible and very moving. It's one of the finest poems ever to explore the father–son relationship – about which Arnold knew a good deal. What Freud would have made of the poem one would like to know, since it tells of a son being killed by a father.

It is common enough for poets in 'the middle stretch' (as Louis MacNeice called it) to have a crisis of confidence, to start doubting whether the Scholar-Gipsy's 'spark from heaven' will ever fall. In our own times the usual result is that they turn to writing novels, which pay better and at least get some attention. Matthew Arnold didn't write a novel, but on the strength of his Preface he did find himself being asked to write a fair amount of prose. Arnold's problem was that he thought so much about his chosen art – what it was for, how it should develop – that he was often paralysed when it came to writing verse. Nor was he helped by reviews such as Harriet Martineau's, who said 'he was not born a poet, and therefore never can be one'. Nevertheless, he had many mighty projects in mind, such as a Lucretius epic and a tragedy about the end of the Roman Republic. New work did emerge and was collected in *Poems: Second Series* (1854), which also restored some of the poems he had culled earlier, although there were still only short extracts from 'Empedocles on Etna' (Ian Hamilton calls Arnold a bibliographer's nightmare). Most impressive were the five hundred lines of 'Balder Dead' which, partly inspired by Carlyle's interest in the subject, draws on Norse mythology, surprisingly neglected up until then by English poets.

Even as he was lamenting the folly of 'marriage with a narrow income and precarious future' and dreaming of escape somewhere abroad or simply to his beloved Athenaeum club, his fortunes changed: he was elected in May 1857 as the next Professor of Poetry at Oxford. The lectures he gave – after a weak and ill-attended initial event – remain among his finest achievements, especially 'On Translating Homer'. This Oxford success also spurred him on to write *Merope*, a verse drama in the manner of Sophocles (although it was more the example of Goethe who seems to have been in his mind). *Merope* proved no more stageable than any of the plays written by Victorian poets, and both friends and critics panned it unmercifully.

Arnold could not escape the world of education (neither could his siblings, most of whom worked in the field), but it had its advantages. He was invited on a tour of Europe to see how other countries educated their young; the experience moved him to take up the cudgels on behalf of educational reform. Thomas Arnold would surely have approved. In his latter years, the great educationalist's son did not write very much poetry, although there were worthy verses composed with a clear moral purpose. Events touching his family could stir the muse more memorably. The publication of *Tom Brown's Schooldays* sent Matthew (who liked the book) leaping to his father's defence, and sparked the elegy 'Rugby Chapel' (dated November 1857 but probably composed later). The loss of his brother William led to the poem 'A Southern Night'. Other works include 'Heine's Grave' and a return to Obermann and Marguerite ('Obermann Once More', 'The Terrace at Berne'). Some of these didn't quite make the cut for this selection; but I have included the late 'Growing Old', a sardonic rejoinder to Browning's 'Grow old along with me/The best is yet to be'. The major poem of the 1860s, 'Thyrsis', was written after the death of Clough. A sequel to 'The Scholar-Gipsy', it is 'an elegy for a dead friend, but it is also an elegy for Arnold's own aspirations as a poet' – those are Ian Hamilton's words, from his biography, *A Gift Imprisoned*, whose title draws on W.H. Auden's poem about Arnold, observing that he 'thrust his gift in prison till it died'.

1867 saw publication of *New Poems*, which even featured at last the full text of 'Empedocles on Etna', and when Arnold was still only forty-six there was a two-volume *Collected*, involving much revision and adjustment. But in the end it was his prose, especially *Culture and Anarchy* (1869), that would be most influential on future generations. Matthew and Lucy's last years were darkened by the deaths of their sons – two in 1868 and the third in 1872. The poet in him died at much the same time, although he lived until 1888 (the year of T.S. Eliot's birth), and his grave may be seen at All Saints, Laleham.

My poem about his final day, 'Matthew Arnold's Essays', appears in the appendix. I can only imagine how those eyebrows would have reacted to such a tribute, especially one in hendecasyllabics.

JOHN GREENING
Cambridgeshire, Spring 2025

TRUE TO ONE ANOTHER

For my parents

Mycerinus

'Not by the justice that my father spurned,
Not for the thousands whom my father slew,
Altars unfed and temples overturned,
Cold hearts and thankless tongues, where thanks are due;
Fell this dread voice from lips that cannot lie,
Stern sentence of the Powers of Destiny.

'I will unfold my sentence and my crime.
My crime – that, rapt in reverential awe,
I sate obedient, in the fiery prime
Of youth, self-governed, at the feet of Law;
Ennobling this dull pomp, the life of kings,
By contemplation of diviner things.

'My father loved injustice, and lived long;
Crowned with grey hairs he died, and full of sway.
I loved the good he scorned, and hated wrong –
The Gods declare my recompense today.
I looked for life more lasting, rule more high;
And when six years are measured, lo, I die!

'Yet surely, O my people, did I deem
Man's justice from the all-just Gods was given;
A light that from some upper fount did beam,
Some better archetype, whose seat was heaven;
A light that, shining from the blest abodes,
Did shadow somewhat of the life of Gods.

'Mere phantoms of man's self-tormenting heart,
Which on the sweets that woo it dares not feed!
Vain dreams, which quench our pleasures, then depart,
When the duped soul, self-mastered, claims its meed;
When, on the strenuous just man, Heaven bestows,
Crown of his struggling life, an unjust close!

'Seems it so light a thing, then, austere powers,
To spurn man's common lure, life's pleasant things?
Seems there no joy in dances crowned with flowers,
Love free to range, and regal banquetings?
Bend ye on these indeed an unmoved eye,
Not gods, but ghosts, in frozen apathy?

'Or is it that some Force, too stern, too strong,
Even for yourselves to conquer or beguile,
Sweeps earth and heaven and men and gods along,
Like the broad volume of the insurgent Nile?
And the great powers we serve, themselves may be
Slaves of a tyrannous necessity?

'Or in mid-heaven, perhaps, your golden cars,
Where earthly voice climbs never, wing their flight,
And in wild hunt, through mazy tracts of stars,
Sweep in the sounding stillness of the night?
Or in deaf ease, on thrones of dazzling sheen,
Drinking deep draughts of joy, ye dwell serene?

'Oh, wherefore cheat our youth, if thus it be,
Of one short joy, one lust, one pleasant dream?
Stringing vain words of powers we cannot see,

Blind divinations of a will supreme;
Lost labour! when the circumambient gloom
But hides, if Gods, Gods careless of our doom?

'The rest I give to joy. Even while I speak,
My sand runs short; and – as yon star-shot ray,
Hemmed by two banks of cloud, peers pale and weak,
Now, as the barrier closes, dies away –
Even so do past and future intertwine,
Blotting this six years' space, which yet is mine.

'Six years – six little years – six drops of time!
Yet suns shall rise, and many moons shall wane,
And old men die, and young men pass their prime,
And languid pleasure fade and flower again,
And the dull gods behold, ere these are flown,
Revels more deep, joy keener than their own.

'Into the silence of the groves and woods
I will go forth; though something would I say –
Something – yet what, I know not: for the Gods
The doom they pass revoke not nor delay;
And prayers, and gifts, and tears, are fruitless all,
And the night waxes, and the shadows fall.

'Ye men of Egypt, ye have heard your king!
I go, and I return not. But the will
Of the great Gods is plain; and ye must bring
Ill deeds, ill passions, zealous to fulfil
Their pleasure, to their feet; and reap their praise,
The praise of Gods, rich boon! and length of days.'

– So spake he, half in anger, half in scorn;
And one loud cry of grief and of amaze
Broke from his sorrowing people; so he spake,
And turning, left them there; and with brief pause,
Girt with a throng of revellers, bent his way
To the cool region of the groves he loved.
There by the riverbanks he wandered on,
From palm grove on to palm grove, happy trees,
Their smooth tops shining sunward, and beneath
Burying their unsunned stems in grass and flowers;
Where in one dream the feverish time of youth
Might fade in slumber, and the feet of joy
Might wander all day long and never tire.
Here came the king, holding high feast, at morn,
Rose-crowned; and ever, when the sun went down,
A hundred lamps beamed in the tranquil gloom,
From tree to tree all through the twinkling grove,
Revealing all the tumult of the feast –
Flushed guests, and golden goblets foamed with wine;
While the deep-burnished foliage overhead
Splintered the silver arrows of the moon.

  It may be that sometimes his wondering soul
From the loud, joyful laughter of his lips
Might shrink half startled, like a guilty man
Who wrestles with his dream; as some pale shape,
Gliding half hidden through the dusky stems,
Would thrust a hand before the lifted bowl,
Whispering, *A little space, and thou art mine!*
It may be on that joyless feast his eye
Dwelt with mere outward seeming; he, within,
Took measure of his soul, and knew its strength,

And by that silent knowledge, day by day,
Was calmed, ennobled, comforted, sustained.
It may be; but not less his brow was smooth,
And his clear laugh fled ringing through the gloom,
And his mirth quailed not at the mild reproof
Sighed out by winter's sad tranquillity;
Nor, palled with its own fullness, ebbed and died
In the rich languor of long summer days;
Nor withered when the palm-tree plumes, that roofed
With their mild dark his grassy banquet hall,
Bent to the cold winds of the showerless spring;
No, nor grew dark when autumn brought the clouds.

  So six long years he revelled, night and day.
And when the mirth waxed loudest, with dull sound
Sometimes from the grove's centre echoes came,
To tell his wondering people of their king;
In the still night, across the steaming flats,
Mixed with the murmur of the moving Nile.

                        1843–44, with some later revisions

A Question

TO FAUSTA

Joy comes and goes, hope ebbs and flows
    Like the wave;
Change doth unknit the tranquil strength of men.
    Love lends life a little grace,
    A few sad smiles; and then
    Both are laid in one cold place,
        In the grave.

Dreams dawn and fly, friends smile and die
    Like spring flowers;
Our vaunted life is one long funeral.
    Men dig graves with bitter tears
    For their dead hopes; and all,
    Mazed with doubts and sick with fears,
        Count the hours.

We count the hours! These dreams of ours,
    False and hollow,
Do we go hence, and find they are not dead?
    Joys we dimly apprehend
    Faces that smiled and fled,
    Hopes born here, and born to end,
        Shall we follow?

(?) 1844

Shakespeare

Others abide our question. Thou art free.
We ask and ask – Thou smilest and art still,
Out-topping knowledge. For the loftiest hill,
Who to the stars uncrowns his majesty,

Planting his steadfast footsteps in the sea,
Making the heaven of heavens his dwelling place,
Spares but the cloudy border of his base
To the foiled searching of mortality;

And thou, who didst the stars and sunbeams know,
Self-schooled, self-scanned, self-honoured, self-secure,
Didst tread on earth unguessed at. Better so!

All pains the immortal spirit must endure,
All weakness which impairs, all griefs which bow,
Find their sole speech in that victorious brow.

1844

In Utrumque Paratus

If, in the silent mind of One all-pure,
    At first imagined lay
The sacred world; and by procession sure
From those still deeps, in form and colour dressed,
Seasons alternating, and night and day,
The long-mused thought to north, south, east and west,
    Took then its all-seen way;

O waking on a world which thus-wise springs!
    Whether it needs thee count
Betwixt thy waking and the birth of things
Ages or hours – O waking on life's stream!
By lonely pureness to the all-pure fount
(Only by this thou canst) the coloured dream
    Of life remount!

Thin, thin the pleasant human noises grow,
And faint the city gleams;
Rare the lone pastoral huts – marvel not thou!
The solemn peaks but to the stars are known,
But to the stars, and the cold lunar beams;
Alone the sun rises, and alone
    Spring the great streams.

But, if the wild unfathered mass no birth
    In divine seats hath known;
In the blank, echoing solitude if Earth,

Rocking her obscure body to and fro,
Ceases not from all time to heave and groan,
Unfruitful oft, and at her happiest throe
    Forms, what she forms, alone;

O seeming sole to awake, thy sun-bathed head
    Piercing the solemn cloud
Round thy still dreaming brother-world outspread!
O man, whom Earth, thy long-vexed mother, bare
Not without joy – so radiant, so endowed
(Such happy issue crowned her painful care) –
    Be not too proud!

Oh when most self-exalted most alone,
    Chief dreamer, own thy dream!
Thy brother-world stirs at thy feet unknown;
Who hath a monarch's hath no brother's part;
Yet doth thine inmost soul with yearning teem.
– Oh, what a spasm shakes the dreamer's heart!
    '*I, too, but seem.*'

1846

from *Resignation*

TO FAUSTA

We left, just ten years since, you say,
That wayside inn we left today.
Our jovial host, as forth we fare,
Shouts greeting from his easy chair.
High on a bank our leader stands,
Reviews and ranks his motley bands,
Makes clear our goal to every eye –
The valley's western boundary.
A gate swings to! our tide hath flowed
Already from the silent road.
The valley pastures, one by one,
Are threaded, quiet in the sun;
And now, beyond the rude stone bridge,
Slopes gracious up the western ridge.
Its woody border, and the last
Of its dark upland farms, is past –
Cool farms, with open-lying stores,
Under their burnished sycamores;
All past! and through the trees we glide
Emerging on the green hill-side.
There climbing hangs, a far-seen sign,
Our wavering, many-coloured line;
There winds, upstreaming slowly still
Over the summit of the hill.
And now, in front, behold outspread

Those upper regions we must tread!
Mild hollows, and clear heathy swells,
The cheerful silence of the fells.
Some two hours' march, with serious air,
Through the deep noontide heats we fare;
The red grouse, springing at our sound,
Skims, now and then, the shining ground;
No life, save his and ours, intrudes
Upon these breathless solitudes.
Oh, joy! again the farms appear.
Cool shade is there, and rustic cheer;
There springs the brook will guide us down,
Bright comrade, to the noisy town.
Lingering, we follow down; we gain
The town, the highway and the plain.
And many a mile of dusty way,
Parched and road-worn, we made that day;
But, Fausta, I remember well,
That as the balmy darkness fell
We bathed our hands with speechless glee,
That night, in the wide-glimmering sea.

Once more we tread this selfsame road,
Fausta, which ten years since we trod;
Alone we tread it, you and I,
Ghosts of that boisterous company.
Here, where the brook shines, near its head,
In its clear, shallow, turf-fringed bed;
Here, whence the eye first sees, far down,
Capped with faint smoke, the noisy town;
Here sit we, and again unroll,

Though slowly, the familiar whole.
The solemn wastes of heathy hill
Sleep in the July sunshine still;
The selfsame shadows now, as then,
Play through this grassy upland glen;
The loose dark stones on the green way
Lie strewn, it seems, where then they lay;
On this mild bank above the stream
(You crush them!) the blue gentians gleam.
Still this wild brook, the rushes cool,
The sailing foam, the shining pool!
These are not changed; and we, you say,
Are scarce more changed, in truth, than they.

The Gipsies, whom we met below,
They too have long roamed to and fro;
They ramble, leaving, where they pass,
Their fragments on the cumbered grass.
And often to some kindly place
Chance guides the migratory race,
Where, though long wanderings intervene,
They recognise a former scene.
The dingy tents are pitched; the fires
Give to the wind their wavering spires;
In dark knots crouch round the wild flame
Their children, as when first they came;
They see their shackled beasts again
Move, browsing, up the grey-walled lane.
Signs are not wanting, which might raise
The ghost in them of former days –
Signs are not wanting, if they would;

Suggestions to disquietude.
For them, for all, time's busy touch,
While it mends little, troubles much.
Their joints grow stiffer – but the year
Runs his old round of dubious cheer;
Chilly they grow – yet winds in March,
Still, sharp as ever, freeze and parch;
They must live still – and yet, God knows,
Crowded and keen the country grows;
It seems as if, in their decay,
The law grew stronger every day.
So might they reason, so compare,
Fausta, times past with times that are.
But no! – they rubbed through yesterday
In their hereditary way,
And they will rub through, if they can,
Tomorrow on the selfsame plan,
Till death arrive to supersede,
For them, vicissitude and need.

The poet, to whose mighty heart
Heaven doth a quicker pulse impart,
Subdues that energy to scan
Not his own course, but that of man.
Though he move mountains, though his day
Be passed on the proud heights of sway,
Though he hath loosed a thousand chains,
Though he hath borne immortal pains,
Action and suffering though he know –
He hath not lived, if he lives so.
He sees, in some great-historied land,

A ruler of the people stand,
Sees his strong thought in fiery flood
Roll through the heaving multitude;
Exults — yet for no moment's space
Envies the all-regarded place.
Beautiful eyes meet his — and he
Bears to admire uncravingly;
They pass — he, mingled with the crowd,
Is in their far-off triumphs proud.
From some high station he looks down,
At sunset, on a populous town;
Surveys each happy group which fleets,
Toil ended, through the shining streets,
Each with some errand of its own —
And does not say: *I am alone.*
He sees the gentle stir of birth
When morning purifies the earth;
He leans upon a gate, and sees
The pastures, and the quiet trees.
Low, woody hill, with gracious bound,
Folds the still valley almost round;
The cuckoo, loud on some high lawn,
Is answered from the depth of dawn;
In the hedge straggling to the stream,
Pale, dew-drenched, half-shut roses gleam.
But, where the farther side slopes down,
He sees the drowsy new-waked clown
In his white quaint-embroidered frock
Make, whistling, toward his mist-wreathed flock —
Slowly, behind his heavy tread,
The wet, flowered grass heaves up its head.

Leaned on his gate, he gazes – tears
Are in his eyes, and in his ears
The murmur of a thousand years.
Before him he sees life unroll,
A placid and continuous whole –
That general life, which does not cease,
Whose secret is not joy, but peace;
That life, whose dumb wish is not missed
If birth proceeds, if things subsist;
The life of plants, and stones, and rain,
The life he craves – if not in vain
Fate gave, what chance shall not control,
His sad lucidity of soul.

1843–49

The Forsaken Merman

Come, dear children, let us away;
Down and away below!
Now my brothers call from the bay,
Now the great winds shoreward blow,
Now the salt tides seaward flow;
Now the wild white horses play,
Champ and chafe and toss in the spray.
Children dear, let us away!
This way, this way!

Call her once before you go –
Call once yet!
In a voice that she will know:
'Margaret! Margaret!'
Children's voices should be dear
(Call once more) to a mother's ear;
Children's voices, wild with pain –
Surely she will come again!
Call her once and come away;
This way, this way!
'Mother dear, we cannot stay!
The wild white horses foam and fret.'
Margaret! Margaret!

Come, dear children, come away down;
Call no more!
One last look at the white-walled town,

And the little grey church on the windy shore;
Then come down!
She will not come, though you call all day;
Come away, come away!
Children dear, was it yesterday
We heard the sweet bells over the bay?
In the caverns where we lay,
Through the surf and through the swell,
The far-off sound of a silver bell?
Sand-strewn caverns, cool and deep,
Where the winds are all asleep;
Where the spent lights quiver and gleam,
Where the salt weed sways in the stream,
Where the sea beasts, ranged all round,
Feed in the ooze of their pasture ground;
Where the sea snakes coil and twine,
Dry their mail and bask in the brine;
Where great whales come sailing by,
Sail and sail, with unshut eye,
Round the world for ever and aye?
When did music come this way?
Children dear, was it yesterday?

Children dear, was it yesterday
(Call yet once) that she went away?
Once she sat with you and me,
On a red-gold throne in the heart of the sea,
And the youngest sat on her knee.
She combed its bright hair, and she tended it well,
When down swung the sound of a far-off bell.
She sighed, she looked up through the clear green sea;

She said: 'I must go, for my kinsfolk pray
In the little grey church on the shore today.
'Twill be Easter time in the world – ah me!
And I lose my poor soul, Merman! here with thee.'
I said: 'Go up, dear heart, through the waves;
Say thy prayer, and come back to the kind sea caves!'
She smiled, she went up through the surf in the bay.
Children dear, was it yesterday?

Children dear, were we long alone?
'The sea grows stormy, the little ones moan;
Long prayers,' I said, 'in the world they say;
Come!' I said; and we rose through the surf in the bay.
We went up the beach, by the sandy down
Where the sea-stocks bloom, to the white-walled town;
Through the narrow paved streets, where all was still,
To the little grey church on the windy hill.
From the church came a murmur of folk at their prayers,
But we stood without in the cold blowing airs.
We climbed on the graves, on the stones worn with rains,
And we gazed up the aisle through the small leaded panes.
She sat by the pillar; we saw her clear:
'Margaret, hist! come quick, we are here!
Dear heart,' I said, 'we are long alone;
The sea grows stormy, the little ones moan.'
But, ah, she gave me never a look,
For her eyes were sealed to the holy book!
Loud prays the priest; shut stands the door.
Come away, children, call no more!
Come away, come down, call no more!

Down, down, down!
Down to the depths of the sea!
She sits at her wheel in the humming town,
Singing most joyfully.
Hark what she sings: 'O joy, O joy,
For the humming street, and the child with its toy!
For the priest, and the bell, and the holy well;
For the wheel where I spun,
And the blessed light of the sun!'
And so she sings her fill,
Singing most joyfully,
Till the spindle drops from her hand,
And the whizzing wheel stands still.
She steals to the window, and looks at the sand,
And over the sand at the sea;
And her eyes are set in a stare;
And anon there breaks a sigh,
And anon there drops a tear,
From a sorrow-clouded eye,
And a heart sorrow-laden,
A long, long sigh;
For the cold strange eyes of a little Mermaiden
And the gleam of her golden hair.

Come away, away children;
Come, children, come down!
The hoarse wind blows coldly;
Lights shine in the town.
She will start from her slumber
When gusts shake the door;
She will hear the winds howling,

Will hear the waves roar.
We shall see, while above us
The waves roar and whirl,
A ceiling of amber,
A pavement of pearl.
Singing: 'Here came a mortal,
But faithless was she!
And alone dwell for ever
The kings of the sea.'

But, children, at midnight,
When soft the winds blow,
When clear falls the moonlight,
When spring tides are low;
When sweet airs come seaward
From heaths starred with broom,
And high rocks throw mildly
On the blanched sands a gloom;
Up the still, glistening beaches,
Up the creeks we will hie,
Over banks of bright seaweed
The ebb-tide leaves dry.
We will gaze, from the sand-hills,
At the white sleeping town;
At the church on the hill-side –
And then come back down,
Singing: 'There dwells a loved one,
But cruel is she!
She left lonely for ever
The kings of the sea.'

(?) 1847–49

To a Republican Friend, 1848

God knows it, I am with you. If to prize
Those virtues, prized and practised by too few,
But prized, but loved, but eminent in you,
Man's fundamental life; if to despise

The barren optimistic sophistries
Of comfortable moles, whom what they do
Teaches the limit of the just and true
(And for such doing they require not eyes);

If sadness at the long heart-wasting show
Wherein Earth's great ones are disquieted;
If thoughts, not idle, while before me flow

The armies of the homeless and unfed —
If these are yours, if this is what you are,
Then am I yours, and what you feel, I share.

(?) March, 1848

Quiet Work

One lesson, Nature, let me learn of thee,
One lesson which in every wind is blown,
One lesson of two duties kept at one
Though the loud world proclaim their enmity –

Of toil unsevered from tranquillity!
Of labour, that in lasting fruit outgrows
Far noisier schemes, accomplished in repose,
Too great for haste, too high for rivalry!

Yes, while on Earth a thousand discords ring,
Man's fitful uproar mingling with his toil,
Still do thy quiet ministers move on,

Their glorious tasks in silence perfecting;
Still working, blaming still our vain turmoil,
Labourers that shall not fail, when man is gone.

(?) 1848

Switzerland

MEETING

Again I see my bliss at hand,
The town, the lake, are here;
My Marguerite smiles upon the strand,
Unaltered with the year.

I know that graceful figure fair,
That cheek of languid hue;
I know that soft, enkerchiefed hair,
And those sweet eyes of blue.

Again I spring to make my choice;
Again in tones of ire
I hear a God's tremendous voice:
'Be counselled, and retire.'

Ye guiding Powers who join and part,
What would ye have with me?
Ah, warn some more ambitious heart,
And let the peaceful be!

PARTING

Ye storm winds of autumn!
Who rush by, who shake
The window, and ruffle
The gleam-lighted lake;
Who cross to the hill-side
Thin-sprinkled with farms,
Where the high woods strip sadly
Their yellowing arms –
Ye are bound for the mountains!
Ah! with you let me go
Where your cold, distant barrier,
The vast range of snow,
Through the loose clouds lifts dimly
Its white peaks in air –
How deep is their stillness!
Ah, would I were there!

But on the stairs what voice is this I hear,
Buoyant as morning, and as morning clear?
Say, has some wet bird-haunted English lawn
Lent it the music of its trees at dawn?
Or was it from some sun-flecked mountain brook
That the sweet voice its upland clearness took?
      Ah! it comes nearer –
      Sweet notes, this way!

Hark! fast by the window
The rushing winds go,

> To the ice-cumbered gorges,
> The vast seas of snow!
> There the torrents drive upward
> Their rock-strangled hum;
> There the avalanche thunders
> The hoarse torrent dumb.
> – I come, O ye mountains!
> Ye torrents, I come!

But who is this, by the half-opened door,
Whose figure casts a shadow on the floor?
The sweet blue eyes – the soft, ash-coloured hair –
The cheeks that still their gentle paleness wear –
The lovely lips, with their arch smile that tells
The unconquered joy in which her spirit dwells –
> Ah! they bend nearer –
> Sweet lips, this way!

> Hark! the wind rushes past us!
> Ah! with that let me go
> To the clear, waning hill-side,
> Unspotted by snow,
> There to watch, o'er the sunk vale,
> The frore mountain-wall,
> Where the niched snow bed sprays down
> Its powdery fall.
> There its dusky blue clusters
> The aconite spreads;
> There the pines slope, the cloud-strips
> Hung soft in their heads.

No life but, at moments,
The mountain bee's hum.
– I come, O ye mountains!
Ye pinewoods, I come!

Forgive me! forgive me!
    Ah, Marguerite, fain
Would these arms reach to clasp thee!
    But see! 'tis in vain.

In the void air, towards thee,
    My stretched arms are cast;
But a sea rolls between us –
    Our different past!

To the lips, ah! of others
    Those lips have been pressed,
And others, ere I was,
    Were strained to that breast.

Far, far from each other
    Our spirits have grown;
And what heart knows another?
    Ah! who knows his own?

Blow, ye winds! lift me with you!
    I come to the wild.
Fold closely, O Nature!
    Thine arms round thy child.

To thee only God granted
    A heart ever new —
To all always open,
    To all always true.

Ah! calm me, restore me;
    And dry up my tears
On thy high mountain-platforms,
    Where morn first appears;

Where the white mists, for ever,
    Are spread and upfurled —
In the stir of the forces
    Whence issued the world.

ISOLATION. TO MARGUERITE

We were apart: yet, day by day,
I bade my heart more constant be.
I bade it keep the world away,
And grow a home for only thee;
Nor feared but thy love likewise grew,
Like mine, each day, more tried, more true.

The fault was grave! I might have known,
What far too soon, alas! I learned –
The heart can bind itself alone,
And faith may oft be unreturned.
Self-swayed our feelings ebb and swell –
Thou lov'st no more – Farewell! Farewell!

Farewell! – and thou, thou lonely heart,
Which never yet without remorse
Even for a moment didst depart
From thy remote and spherèd course
To haunt the place where passions reign –
Back to thy solitude again!

Back! with the conscious thrill of shame
Which Luna felt, that summer night,
Flash through her pure immortal frame,
When she forsook the starry height
To hang over Endymion's sleep
Upon the pine-grown Latmian steep.

Yet she, chaste queen, had never proved
How vain a thing is mortal love,
Wandering in heaven, far removed.
But thou hast long had place to prove
This truth — to prove, and make thine own:
'Thou hast been, shalt be, art, alone.'

Or, if not quite alone, yet they
Which touch thee are unmating things —
Ocean and clouds and night and day;
Lorn autumns and triumphant springs;
And life, and others' joy and pain,
And love, if love, of happier men.

Of happier men — for they, at least,
Have *dreamed* two human hearts might blend
In one, and were through faith released
From isolation without end
Prolonged; nor knew, although not less
Alone than thou, their loneliness.

TO MARGUERITE — CONTINUED

Yes! in the sea of life enisled,
With echoing straits between us thrown,
Dotting the shoreless watery wild,
We mortal millions live *alone*.
The islands feel the enclasping flow,
And then their endless bounds they know.

But when the moon their hollows lights,
And they are swept by balms of spring,
And in their glens, on starry nights,
The nightingales divinely sing;
And lovely notes, from shore to shore,
Across the sounds and channels pour —

Oh! then a longing like despair
Is to their farthest caverns sent;
For surely once, they feel, we were
Parts of a single continent!
Now round us spreads the watery plain —
Oh, might our marges meet again!

Who ordered that their longing's fire
Should be, as soon as kindled, cooled?
Who renders vain their deep desire?
— A God, a God their severance ruled!
And bade betwixt their shores to be
The unplumbed, salt, estranging sea.

A FAREWELL

My horse's feet beside the lake,
Where sweet the unbroken moonbeams lay,
Sent echoes through the night to wake
Each glistening strand, each heath-fringed bay.

The poplar avenue was passed,
And the roofed bridge that spans the stream;
Up the steep street I hurried fast,
Led by thy taper's starlike beam.

I came! I saw thee rise! – the blood
Poured flushing to thy languid cheek.
Locked in each other's arms we stood,
In tears, with hearts too full to speak.

Days flew; ah, soon I could discern
A trouble in thine altered air!
Thy hand lay languidly in mine,
Thy cheek was grave, thy speech grew rare.

I blame thee not! – this heart, I know,
To be long loved was never framed;
For something in its depths doth glow
Too strange, too restless, too untamed.

And women – things that live and move
Mined by the fever of the soul –
They seek to find in those they love
Stern strength, and promise of control.

They ask not kindness, gentle ways –
These they themselves have tried and known;
They ask a soul which never sways
With the blind gusts that shake their own.

I too have felt the load I bore
In a too-strong emotion's sway;
I too have wished, no woman more,
This starting, feverish heart away.

I too have longed for trenchant force,
And will like a dividing spear;
Have praised the keen, unscrupulous course,
Which knows no doubt, which feels no fear.

But in the world I learnt, what there
Thou too wilt surely one day prove,
That will, that energy, though rare,
Are yet far, far less rare than love.

Go, then! – till time and fate impress
This truth on thee, be mine no more!
They will! – for thou, I feel, not less
Than I, wast destined to this lore.

We school our manners, act our parts –
But He, who sees us through and through,
Knows that the bent of both our hearts
Was to be gentle, tranquil, true.

And though we wear out life, alas!
Distracted as a homeless wind,
In beating where we must not pass,
In seeking what we shall not find;

Yet we shall one day gain, life past,
Clear prospect o'er our being's whole;
Shall see ourselves, and learn at last
Our true affinities of soul.

We shall not then deny a course
To every thought the mass ignore;
We shall not then call hardness force,
Nor lightness wisdom any more.

Then, in the eternal Father's smile,
Our soothed, encouraged souls will dare
To seem as free from pride and guile,
As good, as generous, as they are.

Then we shall know our friends! – though much
Will have been lost – the help in strife,
The thousand sweet, still joys of such
As hand in hand face earthly life –

Though these be lost, there will be yet
A sympathy august and pure;
Ennobled by a vast regret,
And by contrition sealed thrice sure.

And we, whose ways were unlike here,
May then more neighbouring courses ply;
May to each other be brought near,
And greet across infinity.

How sweet, unreached by earthly jars,
My sister! to maintain with thee
The hush among the shining stars,
The calm upon the moonlit sea!

How sweet to feel, on the boon air,
All our unquiet pulses cease!
To feel that nothing can impair
The gentleness, the thirst for peace –

The gentleness too rudely hurled
On this wild earth of hate and fear;
The thirst for peace, a raving world
Would never let us satiate here.

ABSENCE

In this fair stranger's eyes of grey,
Thine eyes, my love! I see.
I shiver; for the passing day
Had borne me far from thee.

This is the curse of life! that not
A nobler, calmer train
Of wiser thoughts and feelings blot
Our passions from our brain;

But each day brings its petty dust
Our soon-choked souls to fill,
And we forget because we must,
And not because we will.

I struggle towards the light; and ye,
Once-longed-for storms of love!
If with the light ye cannot be,
I bear that ye remove.

I struggle towards the light – but oh,
While yet the night is chill,
Upon time's barren, stormy flow,
Stay with me, Marguerite, still!

1849

The Terrace at Berne

(COMPOSED TEN YEARS AFTER THE PRECEDING)

Ten years! and to my waking eye
Once more the roofs of Berne appear;
The rocky banks, the terrace high,
The stream! – and do I linger here?

The clouds are on the Oberland,
The Jungfrau snows look faint and far;
But bright are those green fields at hand,
And through those fields comes down the Aar,

And from the blue twin lakes it comes,
Flows by the town, the churchyard fair;
And 'neath the garden-walk it hums,
The house! – and is my Marguerite there?

Ah, shall I see thee, while a flush
Of startled pleasure floods thy brow,
Quick through the oleanders brush,
And clap thy hands, and cry: *'Tis thou!*

Or hast thou long since wandered back,
Daughter of France! to France, thy home;
And flitted down the flowery track
Where feet like thine too lightly come?

Doth riotous laughter now replace
Thy smile; and rouge, with stony glare,
Thy cheek's soft hue, and fluttering lace
The kerchief that enwound thy hair?

Or is it over? – art thou dead?
Dead! – and no warning shiver ran
Across my heart, to say thy thread
Of life was cut, and closed thy span!

Could from Earth's ways that figure slight
Be lost, and I not feel 'twas so?
Of that fresh voice the gay delight
Fail from Earth's air, and I not know?

Or shall I find thee still, but changed,
But not the Marguerite of thy prime?
With all thy being rearranged,
Passed through the crucible of time;

With spirit vanished, beauty waned,
And hardly yet a glance, a tone,
A gesture – anything – retained
Of all that was my Marguerite's own?

I will not know! For wherefore try,
To things by mortal course that live,
A shadowy durability,
For which they were not meant, to give?

Like driftwood spars, which meet and pass
Upon the boundless ocean plain,
So on the sea of life, alas!
Man meets man – meets, and quits again.

I knew it when my life was young;
I feel it still now youth is o'er.
– The mists are on the mountain hung,
And Marguerite I shall see no more.

1863

from *Stanzas in Memory of the Author of* Obermann

Ah! two desires toss about
The poet's feverish blood.
One drives him to the world without,
And one to solitude.

The glow, he cries, *the thrill of life,*
Where, where do these abound?
Not in the world, not in the strife
Of men, shall they be found.

He who hath watched, not shared, the strife
Knows how the day hath gone:
He only lives with the world's life,
Who hath renounced his own.

To thee we come, then! Clouds are rolled
Where thou, O seer! art set;
Thy realm of thought is drear and cold –
The world is colder yet.

And thou hast pleasures, too, to share
With those who come to thee –
Balms floating on thy mountain air,
And healing sights to see.

How often, where the slopes are green
On Jaman, hast thou sate
By some high chalet door, and seen
The summer day grow late;

And darkness steal o'er the wet grass
With the pale crocus starred,
And reach that glimmering sheet of glass
Beneath the piny sward,

Lake Leman's waters, far below.
And watched the rosy light
Fade from the distant peaks of snow;
And on the air of night

Heard accents of the eternal tongue
Through the pine branches play –
Listened, and felt thyself grow young.
Listened, and wept – Away!

Away the dreams that but deceive
And thou, sad guide, adieu!
I go, fate drives me; but I leave
Half of my life with you.

We, in some unknown Power's employ,
Move on a rigorous line;
Can neither, when we will, enjoy,
Nor, when we will, resign.

I in the world must live; but thou,
Thou melancholy shade,
Wilt not, if thou canst see me now,
Condemn me, nor upbraid.

For thou art gone away from Earth,
And place with those dost claim,
The Children of the Second Birth,
Whom the world could not tame;

And with that small transfigured band,
Whom many a different way
Conducted to their common land,
Thou learn'st to think as they.

1849

Youth's Agitations

When I shall be divorced, some ten years hence,
From this poor present self which I am now;
When youth has done its tedious vain expense
Of passions that for ever ebb and flow;

Shall I not joy youth's heats are left behind,
And breathe more happy in an even clime?
Ah no, for then I shall begin to find
A thousand virtues in this hated time!

Then I shall wish its agitations back,
And all its thwarting currents of desire;
Then I shall praise the heat which then I lack,
And call this hurrying fever, generous fire;

And sigh that one thing only has been lent
To youth and age in common – discontent.

1849

from *Empedocles on Etna*

CALLICLES' SONG

The track winds down to the clear stream,
To cross the sparkling shallows; there
The cattle love to gather, on their way
To the high mountain pastures, and to stay,
Till the rough cowherds drive them past,
Knee-deep in the cool ford; for 'tis the last
Of all the woody, high, well-watered dells
On Etna; and the beam
Of noon is broken there by chestnut boughs
Down its steep verdant sides; the air
Is freshened by the leaping stream, which throws
Eternal showers of spray on the mossed roots
Of trees, and veins of turf, and long dark shoots
Of ivy plants, and fragrant hanging bells
Of hyacinths, and on late anemones,
That muffle its wet banks; but glade,
And stream, and sward, and chestnut trees
End here; Etna beyond, in the broad glare
Of the hot noon, without a shade,
Slope behind slope, up to the peak, lies bare;
The peak, round which the white clouds play.

    In such a glen, on such a day,
    On Pelion, on the grassy ground
    Chiron, the aged Centaur, lay,

The young Achilles standing by.
The Centaur taught him to explore
The mountains; where the glens are dry,
And the tired Centaurs come to rest,
And where the soaking springs abound,
And the straight ashes grow for spears,
And where the hill goats come to feed,
And the sea eagles build their nest.
He showed him Phthia far away,
And said: *O boy, I taught this lore*
To Peleus, in long-distant years!
He told him of the Gods, the stars,
The tides; and then of mortal wars,
And of the life which heroes lead
Before they reach the Elysian place
And rest in the immortal mead;
And all the wisdom of his race.

EMPEDOCLES' FINAL SPEECH

But mind, but thought —
If these have been the master part of us —
Where will *they* find their parent element?
What will receive *them*, who will call *them* home?
But we shall still be in them, and they in us,
And we shall be the strangers of the world,
And they will be our lords, as they are now,
And keep us prisoners of our consciousness,
And never let us clasp and feel the All
But through their forms, and modes, and stifling veils.
And we shall be unsatisfied as now;
And we shall feel the agony of thirst,
The ineffable longing for the life of life
Baffled for ever; and still thought and mind
Will hurry us with them on their homeless march
Over the unallied unopening earth,
Over the unrecognising sea; while air
Will blow us fiercely back to sea and earth,
And fire repel us from its living waves.
And then we shall unwillingly return
Back to this meadow of calamity,
This uncongenial place, this human life;
And in our individual human state
Go through the sad probation all again,
To see if we will poise our life at last,
To see if we will now at last be true
To our own only true, deep-buried selves,
Being one with which we are one with the whole world;

Or whether we will once more fall away
Into the bondage of the flesh or mind,
Some slough of sense, or some fantastic maze
Forged by the imperious lonely thinking power.
And each succeeding age in which we are born
Will have more peril for us than the last;
Will goad our senses with a sharper spur,
Will fret our minds to an intenser play,
Will make ourselves harder to be discerned.
And we shall struggle a while, gasp and rebel –
And we shall fly for refuge to past times,
Their soul of unworn youth, their breath of greatness;
And the reality will pluck us back,
Knead us in its hot hand, and change our nature.
And we shall feel our powers of effort flag,
And rally them for one last fight – and fail;
And we shall sink in the impossible strife,
And be astray for ever.

1849

from *Tristram and Iseult*

And is she happy? Does she see unmoved
The days in which she might have lived and loved
Slip without bringing bliss slowly away,
One after one, tomorrow like today?
Joy has not found her yet, nor ever will –
Is it this thought which makes her mien so still,
Her features so fatigued, her eyes, though sweet,
So sunk, so rarely lifted save to meet
Her children's? She moves slow; her voice alone
Hath yet an infantine and silver tone,
But even that comes languidly; in truth,
She seems one dying in a mask of youth.
And now she will go home, and softly lay
Her laughing children in their beds, and play
A while with them before they sleep; and then
She'll light her silver lamp, which fishermen
Dragging their nets through the rough waves, afar,
Along this iron coast, know like a star,
And take her broidery frame, and there she'll sit
Hour after hour, her gold curls sweeping it;
Lifting her soft-bent head only to mind
Her children, or to listen to the wind.
And when the clock peals midnight, she will move
Her work away, and let her fingers rove
Across the shaggy brows of Tristram's hound,
Who lies, guarding her feet, along the ground;

Or else she will fall musing, her blue eyes
Fixed, her slight hands clasped on her lap; then rise,
And at her prie-dieu kneel, until she have told
Her rosary beads of ebony tipped with gold,
Then to her soft sleep – and tomorrow'll be
Today's exact repeated effigy.

                                                    1849

Faded Leaves

THE RIVER

On the broad-bosomed lordly Thames
Down which we glide, the August sun
In mellow evening splendour flames;
Soon will our voyage all be done.

Wrapped in thy shawl, in still repose
Back in the stern seat soft-reclined,
Round thy sweet form the cool air blows,
And thy veil flutters in the wind.

While I, crouched further yet astern,
Wait for the voice that flowed erewhile,
Wait for the graceful head to turn,
And lightly look, and gaily smile.

But ah, the head keeps turned away;
I only see those fingers small
Flit charmingly in careless play
Through the green fringes of thy shawl.

Ah, let the harmless fringes float,
Let the shawl be; for it leaves bare
A lovely strip of thy soft throat
Gleaming between it and thy hair.

And see – for sleep his heavy balms
On all our tired crew outpours –
With half-shut eyes and languid arms
The rowers dip and lift their oars.

Still glides the stream, slow drops the boat
Under the rustling poplars' shade;
Silent the swans beside us float –
None speaks, none heeds; ah, turn thy head!

Let those arch eyes now softly shine,
That mocking mouth grow sweetly bland;
Ah, let them rest, those eyes, on mine!
On mine let rest that lovely hand!

My pent-up tears oppress my brain,
My heart is swollen with love unsaid.
Ah, let me weep, and tell my pain,
And on thy shoulder rest my head!

Before I die – before the soul,
Which now is mine, must re-attain
Immunity from my control,
And wander round the world again;

Before this teased, o'erlaboured heart
For ever leaves its vain employ,
Dead to its deep habitual smart,
And dead to hopes of future joy.

TOO LATE

Each on his own strict line we move,
And some find death ere they find love;
So far apart their lives are thrown
From the twin soul which halves their own.

And sometimes, by still harder fate,
The lovers meet, but meet too late.
– Thy heart is mine! – *True, true! ah, true!*
– Then, love, thy hand! – *Ah, no! adieu!*

SEPARATION

Stop! – not to me, at this bitter departing,
    Speak of the sure consolations of time!
Fresh be the wound, still-renewed be its smarting,
    So but thy image endure in its prime.

But, if the steadfast commandment of Nature
    Wills that remembrance should always decay –
If the loved form and the deep-cherished feature
    Must, when unseen, from the soul fade away –

Me let no half-effaced memories cumber!
    Fled, fled at once, be all vestige of thee!
Deep be the darkness, and still be the slumber –
    Dead be the past and its phantoms to me!

Then, when we meet, and thy look strays toward me,
    Scanning my face and the changes wrought there;
Who, let me say, *is this stranger regards me,*
    With the grey eyes, and the lovely brown hair?

ON THE RHINE

Vain is the effort to forget.
Some day I shall be cold, I know,
As is the eternal moonlit snow
Of the high Alps, to which I go –
But ah! not yet, not yet!

Vain is the agony of grief.
'Tis true, indeed, an iron knot
Ties straitly up from mine thy lot,
And were it snapped – thou lov'st me not!
But is despair relief?

Awhile let me with thought have done.
And as this brimmed unwrinkled Rhine,
And that far purple mountain line,
Lie sweetly in the look divine
Of the slow-sinking sun;

So let me lie, and, calm as they,
Let beam upon my inward view
Those eyes of deep, soft, lucent hue –
Eyes too expressive to be blue,
Too lovely to be grey.

Ah, Quiet, all things feel thy balm!
Those blue hills too, this river's flow,
Were restless once, but long ago.
Tamed is their turbulent youthful glow;
Their joy is in their calm.

LONGING

Come to me in my dreams, and then
By day I shall be well again!
For then the night will more than pay
The hopeless longing of the day.

Come, as thou cam'st a thousand times,
A messenger from radiant climes,
And smile on thy new world, and be
As kind to others as to me!

Or, as thou never cam'st in sooth,
Come now, and let me dream it truth;
And part my hair, and kiss my brow,
And say, *My love! why sufferest thou?*

Come to me in my dreams, and then
By day I shall be well again!
For then the night will more than pay
The hopeless longing of the day.

1849–50

Memorial Verses

APRIL, 1850

Goethe in Weimar sleeps, and Greece,
Long since, saw Byron's struggle cease.
But one such death remained to come;
The last poetic voice is dumb —
We stand today by Wordsworth's tomb.

When Byron's eyes were shut in death,
We bowed our head and held our breath.
He taught us little, but our soul
Had *felt* him like the thunder's roll.
With shivering heart the strife we saw
Of passion with eternal law;
And yet with reverential awe
We watched the fount of fiery life
Which served for that Titanic strife.

   When Goethe's death was told, we said:
Sunk, then, is Europe's sagest head.
Physician of the iron age,
Goethe has done his pilgrimage.
He took the suffering human race,
He read each wound, each weakness clear;
And struck his finger on the place,
And said: *Thou ailest here, and here!*
He looked on Europe's dying hour

Of fitful dream and feverish power;
His eye plunged down the weltering strife,
The turmoil of expiring life –
He said: *The end is everywhere;*
Art still has truth, take refuge there!
And he was happy, if to know
Causes of things, and far below
His feet to see the lurid flow
Of terror, and insane distress,
And headlong fate, be happiness.

And Wordsworth! – Ah, pale ghosts, rejoice!
For never has such soothing voice
Been to your shadowy world conveyed,
Since erst, at morn, some wandering shade
Heard the clear song of Orpheus come
Through Hades, and the mournful gloom.
Wordsworth has gone from us – and ye,
Ah, may ye feel his voice as we!
He too upon a wintry clime
Had fallen – on this iron time
Of doubts, disputes, distractions, fears.
He found us when the age had bound
Our souls in its benumbing round;
He spoke, and loosed our heart in tears.
He laid us as we lay at birth
On the cool flowery lap of earth,
Smiles broke from us, and we had ease;
The hills were round us, and the breeze
Went o'er the sunlit fields again;
Our foreheads felt the wind and rain.

Our youth returned; for there was shed
On spirits that had long been dead,
Spirits dried up and closely furled,
The freshness of the early world.

Ah! since dark days still bring to light
Man's prudence and man's fiery might,
Time may restore us in his course
Goethe's sage mind and Byron's force;
But where will Europe's latter hour
Again find Wordsworth's healing power?
Others will teach us how to dare,
And against fear our breast to steel;
Others will strengthen us to bear —
But who, ah! who will make us feel?
The cloud of mortal destiny,
Others will front it fearlessly —
But who, like him, will put it by?

Keep fresh the grass upon his grave,
O Rotha, with thy living wave!
Sing him thy best! for few or none
Hears thy voice right, now he is gone.

1850

The Youth of Nature

Raised are the dripping oars,
Silent the boat! The lake,
Lovely and soft as a dream,
Swims in the sheen of the moon.
The mountains stand at its head
Clear in the pure June night,
But the valleys are flooded with haze.
Rydal and Fairfield are there;
In the shadow Wordsworth lies dead.
So it is, so it will be for aye.
Nature is fresh as of old,
Is lovely; a mortal is dead.

The spots which recall him survive,
For he lent a new life to these hills.
The Pillar still broods o'er the fields
Which border Ennerdale Lake,
And Egremont sleeps by the sea.
The gleam of the Evening Star
Twinkles on Grasmere no more,
But ruined and solemn and grey
The sheepfold of Michael survives;
And, far to the south, the heath
Still blows in the Quantock coombs,
By the favourite waters of Ruth.
These survive! – yet not without pain,
Pain and dejection tonight,
Can I feel that their poet is gone.

He grew old in an age he condemned.
He looked on the rushing decay
Of the times which had sheltered his youth;
Felt the dissolving throes
Of a social order he loved;
Outlived his brethren, his peers,
And, like the Theban seer,
Died in his enemies' day.

Cold bubbled the spring of Tilphusa,
Copais lay bright in the moon,
Helicon glassed in the lake
Its firs, and afar rose the peaks
Of Parnassus, snowily clear;
Thebes was behind him in flames,
And the clang of arms in his ear,
When his awestruck captors led
The Theban seer to the spring.
Tiresias drank and died.
Nor did reviving Thebes
See such a prophet again.

Well may we mourn, when the head
Of a sacred poet lies low
In an age which can rear them no more!
The complaining millions of men
Darken in labour and pain;
But he was a priest to us all
Of the wonder and bloom of the world,
Which we saw with his eyes, and were glad.

He is dead, and the fruit-bearing day
Of his race is past on the earth;
And darkness returns to our eyes.

For, oh! is it you, is it you,
Moonlight, and shadow, and lake,
And mountains, that fill us with joy,
Or the poet who sings you so well?
Is it you, O beauty, O grace,
O charm, O romance, that we feel,
Or the voice which reveals what you are?
Are ye, like daylight and sun,
Shared and rejoiced in by all?
Or are ye immersed in the mass
Of matter, and hard to extract,
Or sunk at the core of the world
Too deep for the most to discern?
Like stars in the deep of the sky,
Which arise on the glass of the sage,
But are lost when their watcher is gone.

'They are here' – I heard, as men heard
In Mysian Ida the voice
Of the Mighty Mother, or Crete,
The murmur of Nature, reply –
'Loveliness, magic, grace,
They are here! they are set in the world,
They abide; and the finest of souls
Hath not been thrilled by them all,
Nor the dullest been dead to them quite.
The poet who sings them may die,

But they are immortal and live,
For they are the life of the world.
Will ye not learn it, and know,
When ye mourn that a poet is dead,
That the singer was less than his themes,
Life, and emotion, and I?

'More than the singer are these.
Weak is the tremor of pain
That thrills in his mournfullest chord
To that which once ran through his soul.
Cold the elation of joy
In his gladdest, airiest song,
To that which of old in his youth
Filled him and made him divine.
Hardly his voice at its best
Gives us a sense of the awe,
The vastness, the grandeur, the gloom,
Of the unlit gulf of himself.

'Ye know not yourselves; and your bards —
The clearest, the best, who have read
Most in themselves — have beheld
Less than they left unrevealed.
Ye express not yourselves; can you make
With marble, with colour, with word,
What charmed you in others relive?
Can thy pencil, O artist! restore
The figure, the bloom of thy love,
As she was in her morning of spring?
Canst thou paint the ineffable smile

Of her eyes as they rested on thine?
Can the image of life have the glow,
The motion of life itself?

'Yourselves and your fellows ye know not; and me,
The mateless, the one, will ye know?
Will ye scan me, and read me, and tell
Of the thoughts that ferment in my breast,
My longing, my sadness, my joy?
Will ye claim for your great ones the gift
To have rendered the gleam of my skies,
To have echoed the moan of my seas,
Uttered the voice of my hills?
When your great ones depart, will ye say:
All things have suffered a loss,
Nature is hid in their grave?

'Race after race, man after man,
Have thought that my secret was theirs,
Have dreamed that I lived but for them,
That they were my glory and joy.
– They are dust, they are changed, they are gone!
I remain.'

1850–52

Dover Beach

The sea is calm tonight.
The tide is full, the moon lies fair
Upon the straits; on the French coast the light
Gleams and is gone; the cliffs of England stand,
Glimmering and vast, out in the tranquil bay.
Come to the window, sweet is the night air!
Only, from the long line of spray
Where the sea meets the moon-blanched land,
Listen! you hear the grating roar
Of pebbles which the waves draw back, and fling,
At their return, up the high strand,
Begin, and cease, and then again begin,
With tremulous cadence slow, and bring
The eternal note of sadness in.

Sophocles long ago
Heard it on the Aegean, and it brought
Into his mind the turbid ebb and flow
Of human misery; we
Find also in the sound a thought,
Hearing it by this distant northern sea.

The Sea of Faith
Was once, too, at the full, and round Earth's shore
Lay like the folds of a bright girdle furled.
But now I only hear
Its melancholy, long, withdrawing roar,

Retreating, to the breath
Of the night wind, down the vast edges drear
And naked shingles of the world.

Ah, love, let us be true
To one another! for the world, which seems
To lie before us like a land of dreams,
So various, so beautiful, so new,
Hath really neither joy, nor love, nor light,
Nor certitude, nor peace, nor help for pain;
And we are here as on a darkling plain
Swept with confused alarms of struggle and flight,
Where ignorant armies clash by night.

1851

The Buried Life

Light flows our war of mocking words, and yet,
Behold, with tears mine eyes are wet!
I feel a nameless sadness o'er me roll.
Yes, yes, we know that we can jest,
We know, we know that we can smile!
But there's a something in this breast,
To which thy light words bring no rest,
And thy gay smiles no anodyne.
Give me thy hand, and hush awhile,
And turn those limpid eyes on mine,
And let me read there, love! thy inmost soul.

Alas! is even love too weak
To unlock the heart, and let it speak?
Are even lovers powerless to reveal
To one another what indeed they feel?
I knew the mass of men concealed
Their thoughts, for fear that if revealed
They would by other men be met
With blank indifference, or with blame reproved;
I knew they lived and moved
Tricked in disguises, alien to the rest
Of men, and alien to themselves – and yet
The same heart beats in every human breast!

But we, my love! – doth a like spell benumb
Our hearts, our voices? must we too be dumb?

Ah! well for us, if even we,
Even for a moment, can get free
Our heart, and have our lips unchained;
For that which seals them hath been deep-ordained.

Fate, which foresaw
How frivolous a baby man would be —
By what distractions he would be possessed,
How he would pour himself in every strife,
And well-nigh change his own identity —
That it might keep from his capricious play
His genuine self, and force him to obey
Even in his own despite his being's law,
Bade through the deep recesses of our breast
The unregarded river of our life
Pursue with indiscernible flow its way;
And that we should not see
The buried stream, and seem to be
Eddying at large in blind uncertainty,
Though driving on with it eternally.

But often, in the world's most crowded streets,
But often, in the din of strife,
There rises an unspeakable desire
After the knowledge of our buried life;
A thirst to spend our fire and restless force
In tracking out our true, original course;
A longing to inquire
Into the mystery of this heart which beats
So wild, so deep in us — to know
Whence our lives come, and where they go.

And many a man in his own breast then delves,
But deep enough, alas! none ever mines.
And we have been on many thousand lines,
And we have shown, on each, spirit and power;
But hardly have we, for one little hour,
Been on our own line, have we been ourselves –
Hardly had skill to utter one of all
The nameless feelings that course through our breast,
But they course on for ever unexpressed.
And long we try in vain to speak and act
Our hidden self, and what we say and do
Is eloquent, is well – but 'tis not true!
And then we will no more be racked
With inward striving, and demand
Of all the thousand nothings of the hour
Their stupefying power;
Ah, yes, and they benumb us at our call!
Yet still, from time to time, vague and forlorn,
From the soul's subterranean depth upborne
As from an infinitely distant land,
Come airs, and floating echoes, and convey
A melancholy into all our day.

Only – but this is rare –
When a belovèd hand is laid in ours,
When, jaded with the rush and glare
Of the interminable hours,
Our eyes can in another's eyes read clear,
When our world-deafened ear
Is by the tones of a loved voice caressed –
A bolt is shot back somewhere in our breast,

And a lost pulse of feeling stirs again.
The eye sinks inward, and the heart lies plain,
And what we mean, we say, and what we would, we know.
A man becomes aware of his life's flow,
And hears its winding murmur; and he sees
The meadows where it glides, the sun, the breeze.

And there arrives a lull in the hot race
Wherein he doth for ever chase
That flying and elusive shadow, rest.
An air of coolness plays upon his face,
And an unwonted calm pervades his breast;
And then he thinks he knows
The hills where his life rose,
And the sea where it goes.

1849–52

Lines Written in Kensington Gardens

In this lone, open glade I lie,
Screened by deep boughs on either hand;
And at its end, to stay the eye,
Those black-crowned, red-boled pine trees stand!

Birds here make song, each bird has his,
Across the girdling city's hum.
How green under the boughs it is!
How thick the tremulous sheep cries come!

Sometimes a child will cross the glade
To take his nurse his broken toy;
Sometimes a thrush flit overhead
Deep in her unknown day's employ.

Here at my feet what wonders pass!
What endless, active life is here!
What blowing daisies, fragrant grass!
An air-stirred forest, fresh and clear.

Scarce fresher is the mountain sod
Where the tired angler lies, stretched out,
And, eased of basket and of rod,
Counts his day's spoil, the spotted trout.

In the huge world which roars hard by,
Be others happy if they can!
But in my helpless cradle I
Was breathed on by the rural Pan.

I, on men's impious uproar hurled,
Think often, as I hear them rave,
That peace has left the upper world,
And now keeps only in the grave.

Yet here is peace for ever new!
When I who watch them am away,
Still all things in this glade go through
The changes of their quiet day.

Then to their happy rest they pass!
The flowers upclose, the birds are fed,
The night comes down upon the grass,
The child sleeps warmly in his bed.

Calm soul of all things! make it mine
To feel, amid the city's jar,
That there abides a peace of thine,
Man did not make, and cannot mar.

The will to neither strive nor cry,
The power to feel with others give!
Calm, calm me more! nor let me die
Before I have begun to live.

1849–52

The Future

A wanderer is man from his birth.
He was born in a ship
On the breast of the river of Time;
Brimming with wonder and joy,
He spreads out his arms to the light,
Rivets his gaze on the banks of the stream.

As what he sees is, so have his thoughts been.
Whether he wakes
Where the snowy mountainous pass,
Echoing the screams of the eagles,
Hems in its gorges the bed
Of the new-born, clear-flowing stream;
Whether he first sees light
Where the river in gleaming rings
Sluggishly winds through the plain;
Whether in sound of the swallowing sea –
As is the world on the banks,
So is the mind of the man.

   Vainly does each, as he glides,
Fable and dream
Of the lands which the river of Time
Had left ere he woke on its breast,
Or shall reach when his eyes have been closed.
Only the tract where he sails
He wots of; only the thoughts,
Raised by the objects he passes, are his.

Who can see the green Earth any more
As she was by the sources of Time?
Who imagines her fields as they lay
In the sunshine, unworn by the plough?
Who thinks as they thought,
The tribes who then roamed on her breast,
Her vigorous, primitive sons?

What girl
Now reads in her bosom as clear
As Rebekah read, when she sat
At eve by the palm-shaded well?
Who guards in her breast
As deep, as pellucid a spring
Of feeling, as tranquil, as sure?

  What bard,
At the height of his vision, can deem
Of God, of the world, of the soul,
With a plainness as near,
As flashing, as Moses felt,
When he lay in the night by his flock
On the starlit Arabian waste?
Can rise and obey
The beck of the Spirit like him?

This tract which the river of Time
Now flows through with us, is the plain.
Gone is the calm of its earlier shore.
Bordered by cities, and hoarse
With a thousand cries is its stream.

And we on its breast, our minds
Are confused as the cries which we hear,
Changing and shot as the sights which we see.

And we say that repose has fled
For ever the course of the river of Time.
That cities will crowd to its edge
In a blacker, incessanter line;
That the din will be more on its banks,
Denser the trade on its stream,
Flatter the plain where it flows,
Fiercer the sun overhead.
That never will those on its breast
See an ennobling sight,
Drink of the feeling of quiet again.

But what was before us we know not,
And we know not what shall succeed.

Haply, the river of Time –
As it grows, as the towns on its marge
Fling their wavering lights
On a wider, statelier stream –
May acquire, if not the calm
Of its early mountainous shore,
Yet a solemn peace of its own.

And the width of the waters, the hush
Of the grey expanse where he floats,
Freshening its current, and spotted with foam
As it draws to the ocean, may strike

Peace to the soul of the man on its breast –
As the pale waste widens around him,
As the banks fade dimmer away,
As the stars come out, and the night wind
Brings up the stream
Murmurs and scents of the infinite sea.

(?) 1852

A Summer Night

In the deserted, moon-blanched street,
How lonely rings the echo of my feet!
Those windows, which I gaze at, frown,
Silent and white, unopening down,
Repellent as the world; but see,
A break between the housetops shows
The moon! and, lost behind her, fading dim
Into the dewy dark obscurity
Down at the far horizon's rim,
Doth a whole tract of heaven disclose!

And to my mind the thought
Is on a sudden brought
Of a past night, and a far different scene.
Headlands stood out into the moonlit deep
As clearly as at noon;
The spring tide's brimming flow
Heaved dazzlingly between;
Houses, with long white sweep,
Girdled the glistening bay;
Behind, through the soft air,
The blue haze-cradled mountains spread away.
That night was far more fair –
But the same restless pacings to and fro,
And the same vainly throbbing heart was there,
And the same bright, calm moon.

And the calm moonlight seems to say:
Hast thou, then, still the old unquiet breast,
Which neither deadens into rest,
Nor ever feels the fiery glow
That whirls the spirit from itself away,
But fluctuates to and fro,
Never by passion quite possessed,
And never quite benumbed by the world's sway?
And I, I know not if to pray
Still to be what I am, or yield, and be
Like all the other men I see.

For most men in a brazen prison live,
Where, in the sun's hot eye,
With heads bent o'er their toil, they languidly
Their lives to some unmeaning taskwork give,
Dreaming of naught beyond their prison wall.
And as, year after year,
Fresh products of their barren labour fall
From their tired hands, and rest
Never yet comes more near,
Gloom settles slowly down over their breast.
And while they try to stem
The waves of mournful thought by which they are
    pressed,
Death in their prison reaches them,
Unfreed, having seen nothing, still unblest.

And the rest, a few,
Escape their prison, and depart
On the wide ocean of life anew.

There the freed prisoner, where'er his heart
Listeth, will sail;
Nor doth he know how there prevail,
Despotic on that sea,
Trade winds which cross it from eternity.
Awhile he holds some false way, undebarred
By thwarting signs, and braves
The freshening wind and blackening waves.
And then the tempest strikes him; and between
The lightning bursts is seen
Only a driving wreck,
And the pale master on his spar-strewn deck
With anguished face and flying hair,
Grasping the rudder hard,
Still bent to make some port, he knows not where,
Still standing for some false, impossible shore.
And sterner comes the roar
Of sea and wind, and through the deepening gloom
Fainter and fainter wreck and helmsman loom,
And he too disappears, and comes no more.

Is there no life, but these alone?
Madman or slave, must man be one?

Plainness and clearness without shadow of stain!
Clearness divine!
Ye heavens, whose pure dark regions have no sign
Of languor, though so calm, and, though so great,
Are yet untroubled and unpassionate;
Who, though so noble, share in the world's toil,
And, though so tasked, keep free from dust and soil!

I will not say that your mild deeps retain
A tinge, it may be, of their silent pain
Who have longed deeply once, and longed in vain –
But I will rather say that you remain
A world above man's head, to let him see
How boundless might his soul's horizons be,
How vast, yet of what clear transparency!
How it were good to abide there, and breathe free;
How fair a lot to fill
Is left to each man still!

1849–52

Stanzas from the Grande Chartreuse

Through Alpine meadows soft-suffused
With rain, where thick the crocus blows,
Past the dark forges long disused,
The mule track from Saint Laurent goes.
The bridge is crossed, and slow we ride,
Through forest, up the mountainside.

The autumnal evening darkens round,
The wind is up, and drives the rain;
While, hark! far down, with strangled sound
Doth the Dead Guier's stream complain,
Where that wet smoke, among the woods,
Over his boiling cauldron broods.

Swift rush the spectral vapours white
Past limestone scars with ragged pines,
Showing – then blotting from our sight!
Halt – through the cloud-drift something shines!
High in the valley, wet and drear,
The huts of Courrerie appear.

Strike leftward! cries our guide; and higher
Mounts up the stony forest way.
At last the encircling trees retire;
Look! through the showery twilight grey,
What pointed roofs are these advance?
A palace of the Kings of France?

Approach, for what we seek is here!
Alight, and sparely sup, and wait
For rest in this outbuilding near;
Then cross the sward and reach that gate;
Knock; pass the wicket! Thou art come
To the Carthusians' world-famed home.

The silent courts, where night and day
Into their stone-carved basins cold
The splashing icy fountains play –
The humid corridors behold,
Where, ghostlike in the deepening night,
Cowled forms brush by in gleaming white.

The chapel, where no organ's peal
Invests the stern and naked prayer –
With penitential cries they kneel
And wrestle; rising then, with bare
And white uplifted faces stand,
Passing the Host from hand to hand;

Each takes, and then his visage wan
Is buried in his cowl once more.
The cells! – the suffering Son of Man
Upon the wall – the knee-worn floor –
And where they sleep, that wooden bed,
Which shall their coffin be, when dead!

The library, where tract and tome
Not to feed priestly pride are there,
To hymn the conquering march of Rome,

Nor yet to amuse, as ours are!
They paint of souls the inner strife,
Their drops of blood, their death in life.

The garden, overgrown – yet mild,
See, fragrant herbs are flowering there!
Strong children of the Alpine wild
Whose culture is the brethren's care;
Of human tasks their only one,
And cheerful works beneath the sun.

Those halls, too, destined to contain
Each its own pilgrim host of old,
From England, Germany or Spain –
All are before me! I behold
The House, the Brotherhood austere!
– And what am I, that I am here?

For rigorous teachers seized my youth,
And purged its faith, and trimmed its fire,
Showed me the high, white star of Truth,
There bade me gaze, and there aspire.
Even now their whispers pierce the gloom:
What dost thou in this living tomb?

Forgive me, masters of the mind!
At whose behest I long ago
So much unlearnt, so much resigned –
I come not here to be your foe!
I seek these anchorites, not in ruth,
To curse and to deny your truth;

Not as their friend, or child, I speak!
But as, on some far northern strand,
Thinking of his own Gods, a Greek
In pity and mournful awe might stand
Before some fallen Runic stone –
For both were faiths, and both are gone.

Wandering between two worlds, one dead,
The other powerless to be born,
With nowhere yet to rest my head,
Like these, on Earth I wait forlorn.
Their faith, my tears, the world deride –
I come to shed them at their side.

Oh, hide me in your gloom profound,
Ye solemn seats of holy pain!
Take me, cowled forms, and fence me round,
Till I possess my soul again;
Till free my thoughts before me roll,
Not chafed by hourly false control!

For the world cries, your faith is now
But a dead time's exploded dream;
My melancholy, sciolists say,
Is a passed mode, an outworn theme –
As if the world had ever had
A faith, or sciolists been sad!

Ah, if it *be* passed, take away,
At least, the restlessness, the pain;
Be man henceforth no more a prey

To these outdated stings again!
The nobleness of grief is gone –
Ah, leave us not the fret alone!

But – if you cannot give us ease –
Last of the race of them who grieve,
Here leave us to die out with these
Last of the people who believe!
Silent, while years engrave the brow;
Silent – the best are silent now.

Achilles ponders in his tent,
The kings of modern thought are dumb;
Silent they are, though not content,
And wait to see the future come.
They have the grief men had of yore,
But they contend and cry no more.

Our fathers watered with their tears
This sea of time whereon we sail;
Their voices were in all men's ears
Who passed within their puissant hail.
Still the same ocean round us raves,
But we stand mute, and watch the waves.

For what availed it, all the noise
And outcry of the former men?
Say, have their sons achieved more joys?
Say, is life lighter now than then?
The sufferers died, they left their pain –
The pangs which tortured them remain.

What helps it now, that Byron bore,
With haughty scorn which mocked the smart,
Through Europe to the Aetolian shore
The pageant of his bleeding heart?
That thousands counted every groan,
And Europe made his woe her own?

What boots it, Shelley! that the breeze
Carried thy lovely wail away,
Musical through Italian trees
Which fringe thy soft blue Spezzian bay?
Inheritors of thy distress,
Have restless hearts one throb the less?

Or are we easier, to have read,
O Obermann! the sad, stern page,
Which tells us how thou hidd'st thy head
From the fierce tempest of thine age
In the lone brakes of Fontainebleau,
Or chalets near the Alpine snow?

Ye slumber in your silent grave!
The world, which for an idle day
Grace to your mood of sadness gave,
Long since hath flung her weeds away.
The eternal trifler breaks your spell;
But we – we learnt your lore too well!

Years hence, perhaps, may dawn an age,
More fortunate, alas! than we,
Which without hardness will be sage,

And gay without frivolity.
Sons of the world, oh, speed those years;
But, while we wait, allow our tears!

Allow them! We admire with awe
The exulting thunder of your race;
You give the universe your law,
You triumph over time and space!
Your pride of life, your tireless powers,
We laud them, but they are not ours.

We are like children reared in shade
Beneath some old-world abbey wall,
Forgotten in a forest glade,
And secret from the eyes of all.
Deep, deep the greenwood round them waves,
Their abbey, and its close of graves!

But, where the road runs near the stream,
Oft through the trees they catch a glance
Of passing troops in the sun's beam –
Pennon, and plume, and flashing lance!
Forth to the world those soldiers fare,
To life, to cities and to war!

And through the woods, another way,
Faint bugle notes from far are borne,
Where hunters gather, staghounds bay,
Round some old forest lodge at morn.
Gay dames are there, in sylvan green;
Laughter and cries – those notes between!

The banners flashing through the trees
Make their blood dance and chain their eyes;
That bugle music on the breeze
Arrests them with a charmed surprise.
Banner by turns and bugle woo:
Ye shy recluses, follow too!

O children, what do ye reply?
'Action and pleasure, will ye roam
Through these secluded dells to cry
And call us? – but too late ye come!
Too late for us your call ye blow,
Whose bent was taken long ago.

'Long since we pace this shadowed nave;
We watch those yellow tapers shine,
Emblems of hope over the grave,
In the high altar's depth divine;
The organ carries to our ear
Its accents of another sphere.

'Fenced early in this cloistral round
Of reverie, of shade, of prayer,
How should we grow in other ground?
How can we flower in foreign air?
– Pass, banners, pass, and bugles, cease;
And leave our desert to its peace!'

1851–55

Sohrab and Rustum

AN EPISODE

And the first grey of morning filled the east,
And the fog rose out of the Oxus stream.
But all the Tartar camp along the stream
Was hushed, and still the men were plunged in sleep;
Sohrab alone, he slept not; all night long
He had lain wakeful, tossing on his bed;
But when the grey dawn stole into his tent,
He rose, and clad himself, and girt his sword,
And took his horseman's cloak, and left his tent,
And went abroad into the cold wet fog,
Through the dim camp to Peran-Wisa's tent.
  Through the black Tartar tents he passed, which stood
Clustering like beehives on the low flat strand
Of Oxus, where the summer floods o'erflow
When the sun melts the snows in high Pamere;
Through the black tents he passed, o'er that low strand,
And to a hillock came, a little back
From the stream's brink – the spot where first a boat,
Crossing the stream in summer, scrapes the land.
The men of former times had crowned the top
With a clay fort; but that was fallen, and now
The Tartars built there Peran-Wisa's tent,
A dome of laths, and o'er it felts were spread.
And Sohrab came there, and went in, and stood
Upon the thick piled carpets in the tent,

And found the old man sleeping on his bed
Of rugs and felts, and near him lay his arms.
And Peran-Wisa heard him, though the step
Was dulled; for he slept light, an old man's sleep;
And he rose quickly on one arm, and said:

    'Who art thou? for it is not yet clear dawn.
Speak! is there news, or any night alarm?'

    But Sohrab came to the bedside, and said:
'Thou know'st me, Peran-Wisa! it is I.
The sun is not yet risen, and the foe
Sleep; but I sleep not; all night long I lie
Tossing and wakeful, and I come to thee.
For so did King Afrasiab bid me seek
Thy counsel, and to heed thee as thy son,
In Samarcand, before the army marched;
And I will tell thee what my heart desires.
Thou know'st if, since from Ader-baijan first
I came among the Tartars, and bore arms,
I have still served Afrasiab well, and shown,
At my boy's years, the courage of a man.
This too thou know'st, that while I still bear on
The conquering Tartar ensigns through the world,
And beat the Persians back on every field,
I seek one man, one man, and one alone –
Rustum, my father; who I hoped should greet,
Should one day greet, upon some well-fought field,
His not unworthy, not inglorious son.
So I long hoped, but him I never find.
Come then, hear now, and grant me what I ask.
Let the two armies rest today; but I
Will challenge forth the bravest Persian lords
To meet me, man to man; if I prevail,

Rustum will surely hear it; if I fall –
Old man, the dead need no one, claim no kin.
Dim is the rumour of a common fight,
Where host meets host, and many names are sunk;
But of a single combat fame speaks clear.'

   He spoke; and Peran-Wisa took the hand
Of the young man in his, and sighed, and said:

   'O Sohrab, an unquiet heart is thine!
Canst thou not rest among the Tartar chiefs,
And share the battle's common chance with us
Who love thee, but must press for ever first,
In single fight incurring single risk,
To find a father thou hast never seen?
That were far best, my son, to stay with us
Unmurmuring; in our tents, while it is war,
And when 'tis truce, then in Afrasiab's towns.
But if this one desire indeed rules all,
To seek out Rustum – seek him not through fight!
Seek him in peace, and carry to his arms,
O Sohrab, carry an unwounded son!
But far hence seek him, for he is not here.
For now it is not as when I was young,
When Rustum was in front of every fray;
But now he keeps apart, and sits at home,
In Seistan, with Zal, his father old.
Whether that his own mighty strength at last
Feels the abhorred approaches of old age,
Or in some quarrel with the Persian king.
There go! – Thou wilt not? Yet my heart forebodes
Danger or death awaits thee on this field.

Fain would I know thee safe and well, though lost
To us; fain therefore send thee hence in peace
To seek thy father, not seek single fights
In vain; but who can keep the lion's cub
From ravening, and who govern Rustum's son?
Go, I will grant thee what thy heart desires.'

  So said he, and dropped Sohrab's hand, and left
His bed, and the warm rugs whereon he lay;
And o'er his chilly limbs his woollen coat
He passed, and tied his sandals on his feet,
And threw a white cloak round him, and he took
In his right hand a ruler's staff, no sword;
And on his head he set his sheepskin cap,
Black, glossy, curled, the fleece of Kara-Kul;
And raised the curtain of his tent, and called
His herald to his side, and went abroad.

  The sun by this had risen, and cleared the fog
From the broad Oxus and the glittering sands.
And from their tents the Tartar horsemen filed
Into the open plain: so Haman bade –
Haman, who next to Peran-Wisa ruled
The host, and still was in his lusty prime.
From their black tents, long files of horse, they streamed;
As when some grey November morn the files,
In marching order spread, of long-necked cranes
Stream over Casbin and the southern slopes
Of Elburz, from the Aralian estuaries,
Or some frore Caspian reedbed, southward bound
For the warm Persian seaboard – so they streamed.
The Tartars of the Oxus, the King's guard,
First, with black sheepskin caps and with long spears;

Large men, large steeds; who from Bokhara come
And Khiva, and ferment the milk of mares.
Next, the more temperate Toorkmuns of the south,
The Tukas, and the lances of Salore,
And those from Attruck and the Caspian sands;
Light men and on light steeds, who only drink
The acrid milk of camels, and their wells.
And then a swarm of wandering horse, who came
From far, and a more doubtful service owned;
The Tartars of Ferghana, from the banks
Of the Jaxartes, men with scanty beards
And close-set skullcaps; and those wilder hordes
Who roam o'er Kipchak and the northern waste,
Kalmucks and unkempt Kuzzaks, tribes who stray
Nearest the Pole, and wandering Kirghizzes,
Who come on shaggy ponies from Pamere;
These all filed out from camp into the plain.
And on the other side the Persians formed;
First a light cloud of horse, Tartars they seemed,
The Ilyats of Khorassan; and behind,
The royal troops of Persia, horse and foot,
Marshalled battalions bright in burnished steel.
But Peran-Wisa with his herald came,
Threading the Tartar squadrons to the front,
And with his staff kept back the foremost ranks.
And when Ferood, who led the Persians, saw
That Peran-Wisa kept the Tartars back,
He took his spear, and to the front he came,
And checked his ranks, and fixed them where they stood.
And the old Tartar came upon the sand
Betwixt the silent hosts, and spake, and said:

'Ferood, and ye, Persians and Tartars, hear!
Let there be truce between the hosts today.
But choose a champion from the Persian lords
To fight our champion Sohrab, man to man.'

As, in the country, on a morn in June,
When the dew glistens on the pearlèd ears,
A shiver runs through the deep corn for joy –
So, when they heard what Peran-Wisa said,
A thrill through all the Tartar squadrons ran
Of pride and hope for Sohrab, whom they loved.

But as a troop of pedlars, from Cabool,
Cross underneath the Indian Caucasus,
That vast sky-neighbouring mountain of milk snow;
Crossing so high, that, as they mount, they pass
Long flocks of travelling birds dead on the snow,
Choked by the air, and scarce can they themselves
Slake their parched throats with sugared mulberries –
In single file they move, and stop their breath,
For fear they should dislodge the o'erhanging snows –
So the pale Persians held their breath with fear.

And to Ferood his brother chiefs came up
To counsel; Gudurz and Zoarrah came,
And Feraburz, who ruled the Persian host
Second, and was the uncle of the King;
These came and counselled, and then Gudurz said:

'Ferood, shame bids us take their challenge up,
Yet champion have we none to match this youth.
He has the wild stag's foot, the lion's heart.
But Rustum came last night; aloof he sits
And sullen, and has pitched his tents apart.
Him will I seek, and carry to his ear
The Tartar challenge, and this young man's name.

Haply he will forget his wrath, and fight.
Stand forth the while, and take their challenge up.'

So spake he; and Ferood stood forth and cried:
'Old man, be it agreed as thou hast said!
Let Sohrab arm, and we will find a man.'

He spake; and Peran-Wisa turned, and strode
Back through the opening squadrons to his tent.
But through the anxious Persians Gudurz ran,
And crossed the camp which lay behind, and reached,
Out on the sands beyond it, Rustum's tents.
Of scarlet cloth they were, and glittering gay,
Just pitched; the high pavilion in the midst
Was Rustum's, and his men lay camped around.
And Gudurz entered Rustum's tent, and found
Rustum; his morning meal was done, but still
The table stood before him, charged with food –
A side of roasted sheep, and cakes of bread,
And dark-green melons; and there Rustum sat
Listless, and held a falcon on his wrist,
And played with it; but Gudurz came and stood
Before him; and he looked, and saw him stand,
And with a cry sprang up, and dropped the bird,
And greeted Gudurz with both hands, and said:

'Welcome! these eyes could see no better sight.
What news? but sit down first, and eat and drink.'

But Gudurz stood in the tent door, and said:
'Not now! a time will come to eat and drink,
But not today: today has other needs.
The armies are drawn out, and stand at gaze;
For from the Tartars is a challenge brought
To pick a champion from the Persian lords

To fight their champion – and thou know'st his name –
Sohrab men call him, but his birth is hid.
O Rustum, like thy might is this young man's!
He has the wild stag's foot, the lion's heart;
And he is young, and Iran's chiefs are old,
Or else too weak; and all eyes turn to thee.
Come down and help us, Rustum, or we lose!'

  He spoke; but Rustum answered with a smile:
'Go to! if Iran's chiefs are old, then I
Am older; if the young are weak, the King
Errs strangely; for the King, for Kai Khosroo,
Himself is young, and honours younger men,
And lets the agèd moulder to their graves.
Rustum he loves no more, but loves the young –
The young may rise at Sohrab's vaunts, not I.
For what care I, though all speak Sohrab's fame?
For would that I myself had such a son,
And not that one slight helpless girl I have –
A son so famed, so brave, to send to war,
And I to tarry with the snow-haired Zal,
My father, whom the robber Afghans vex,
And clip his borders short, and drive his herds,
And he has none to guard his weak old age.
There would I go, and hang my armour up,
And with my great name fence that weak old man,
And spend the goodly treasures I have got,
And rest my age, and hear of Sohrab's fame,
And leave to death the hosts of thankless kings,
And with these slaughterous hands draw sword no more.'

  He spoke, and smiled; and Gudurz made reply:
'What then, O Rustum, will men say to this,

When Sohrab dares our bravest forth, and seeks
Thee most of all, and thou, whom most he seeks,
Hidest thy face? Take heed lest men should say:
Like some old miser, Rustum hoards his fame,
And shuns to peril it with younger men.'

   And, greatly moved, then Rustum made reply:
'O Gudurz, wherefore dost thou say such words?
Thou knowest better words than this to say.
What is one more, one less, obscure or famed,
Valiant or craven, young or old, to me?
Are not they mortal? am not I myself?
But who for men of nought would do great deeds?
Come, thou shalt see how Rustum hoards his fame!
But I will fight unknown, and in plain arms;
Let not men say of Rustum, he was matched
In single fight with any mortal man.'

   He spoke, and frowned; and Gudurz turned, and ran
Back quickly through the camp in fear and joy –
Fear at his wrath, but joy that Rustum came.
But Rustum strode to his tent door, and called
His followers in, and bade them bring his arms,
And clad himself in steel; the arms he chose
Were plain, and on his shield was no device,
Only his helm was rich, inlaid with gold,
And, from the fluted spine atop, a plume
Of horsehair waved, a scarlet horsehair plume.
So armed, he issued forth; and Ruksh, his horse,
Followed him like a faithful hound at heel –
Ruksh, whose renown was noised through all the earth,
The horse whom Rustum on a foray once
Did in Bokhara by the river find
A colt beneath its dam, and drove him home,

And reared him; a bright bay, with lofty crest,
Dight with a saddle-cloth of broidered green
Crusted with gold, and on the ground were worked
All beasts of chase, all beasts which hunters know.
So followed, Rustum left his tents, and crossed
The camp, and to the Persian host appeared.
And all the Persians knew him, and with shouts
Hailed; but the Tartars knew not who he was.
And dear as the wet diver to the eyes
Of his pale wife who waits and weeps on shore,
By sandy Bahrein, in the Persian Gulf,
Plunging all day in the blue waves, at night,
Having made up his tale of precious pearls,
Rejoins her in their hut upon the sands –
So dear to the pale Persians Rustum came.

   And Rustum to the Persian front advanced,
And Sohrab armed in Haman's tent, and came.
And as afield the reapers cut a swathe
Down through the middle of a rich man's corn,
And on each side are squares of standing corn,
And in the midst a stubble short and bare –
So on each side were squares of men, with spears
Bristling, and in the midst, the open sand.
And Rustum came upon the sand, and cast
His eyes toward the Tartar tents, and saw
Sohrab come forth, and eyed him as he came.

   As some rich woman, on a winter's morn,
Eyes through her silken curtains the poor drudge
Who with numb blackened fingers makes her fire –
At cock-crow, on a starlit winter's morn,
When the frost flowers the whitened windowpanes –

And wonders how she lives, and what the thoughts
Of that poor drudge may be; so Rustum eyed
The unknown adventurous youth, who from afar
Came seeking Rustum, and defying forth
All the most valiant chiefs; long he perused
His spirited air, and wondered who he was.
For very young he seemed, tenderly reared;
Like some young cypress, tall, and dark, and straight,
Which in a queen's secluded garden throws
Its slight dark shadow on the moonlit turf,
By midnight, to a bubbling fountain's sound —
So slender Sohrab seemed, so softly reared.
And a deep pity entered Rustum's soul
As he beheld him coming; and he stood,
And beckoned to him with his hand, and said:

'O thou young man, the air of heaven is soft,
And warm, and pleasant; but the grave is cold!
Heaven's air is better than the cold dead grave.
Behold me! I am vast, and clad in iron,
And tried; and I have stood on many a field
Of blood, and I have fought with many a foe —
Never was that field lost, or that foe saved.
O Sohrab, wherefore wilt thou rush on death?
Be governed! quit the Tartar host, and come
To Iran, and be as my son to me,
And fight beneath my banner till I die!
There are no youths in Iran brave as thou.'

So he spake, mildly; Sohrab heard his voice,
The mighty voice of Rustum, and he saw
His giant figure planted on the sand,
Sole, like some single tower, which a chief

Hath builded on the waste in former years
Against the robbers; and he saw that head,
Streaked with its first grey hairs; hope filled his soul,
And he ran forward and embraced his knees,
And clasped his hand within his own, and said:

    'Oh, by thy father's head! by thine own soul!
Art thou not Rustum? speak! art thou not he?'

    But Rustum eyed askance the kneeling youth,
And turned away, and spake to his own soul:

    'Ah me, I muse what this young fox may mean!
False, wily, boastful, are these Tartar boys.
For if I now confess this thing he asks,
And hide it not, but say: *Rustum is here!*
He will not yield indeed, nor quit our foes;
But he will find some pretext not to fight,
And praise my fame, and proffer courteous gifts,
A belt or sword perhaps, and go his way.
And on a feast-tide, in Afrasiab's hall
In Samarcand, he will arise and cry:
'I challenged once, when the two armies camped
Beside the Oxus, all the Persian lords
To cope with me in single fight; but they
Shrank, only Rustum dared; then he and I
Changed gifts, and went on equal terms away.'
So will he speak, perhaps, while men applaud;
Then were the chiefs of Iran shamed through me.'

    And then he turned, and sternly spake aloud:
'Rise! wherefore dost thou vainly question thus
Of Rustum? I am here, whom thou hast called
By challenge forth; make good thy vaunt, or yield!
Is it with Rustum only thou wouldst fight?

Rash boy, men look on Rustum's face and flee!
For well I know, that did great Rustum stand
Before thy face this day, and were revealed,
There would be then no talk of fighting more.
But being what I am, I tell thee this –
Do thou record it in thine inmost soul:
Either thou shalt renounce thy vaunt and yield,
Or else thy bones shall strew this sand, till winds
Bleach them, or Oxus with his summer floods,
Oxus in summer wash them all away.'

  He spoke; and Sohrab answered, on his feet:
'Art thou so fierce? Thou wilt not fright me so!
I am no girl, to be made pale by words.
Yet this thou hast said well, did Rustum stand
Here on this field, there were no fighting then.
But Rustum is far hence, and we stand here.
Begin! thou art more vast, more dread than I,
And thou art proved, I know, and I am young –
But yet success sways with the breath of Heaven.
And though thou thinkest that thou knowest sure
Thy victory, yet thou canst not surely know.
For we are all, like swimmers in the sea,
Poised on the top of a huge wave of fate,
Which hangs uncertain to which side to fall.
And whether it will heave us up to land,
Or whether it will roll us out to sea,
Back out to sea, to the deep waves of death,
We know not, and no search will make us know;
Only the event will teach us in its hour.'

  He spoke, and Rustum answered not, but hurled
His spear; down from the shoulder, down it came,

As on some partridge in the corn a hawk,
That long has towered in the airy clouds,
Drops like a plummet; Sohrab saw it come,
And sprang aside, quick as a flash; the spear
Hissed, and went quivering down into the sand,
Which it sent flying wide; then Sohrab threw
In turn, and full struck Rustum's shield; sharp rang,
The iron plates rang sharp, but turned the spear.
And Rustum seized his club, which none but he
Could wield; an unlopped trunk it was, and huge,
Still rough — like those which men in treeless plains
To build them boats fish from the flooded rivers,
Hyphasis or Hydaspes, when, high up
By their dark springs, the wind in wintertime
Hath made in Himalayan forests wrack,
And strewn the channels with torn boughs — so huge
The club which Rustum lifted now, and struck
One stroke; but again Sohrab sprang aside,
Lithe as the glancing snake, and the club came
Thundering to earth, and leapt from Rustum's hand.
And Rustum followed his own blow, and fell
To his knees, and with his fingers clutched the sand;
And now might Sohrab have unsheathed his sword,
And pierced the mighty Rustum while he lay
Dizzy, and on his knees, and choked with sand;
But he looked on, and smiled, nor bared his sword,
But courteously drew back, and spoke, and said:

  'Thou strik'st too hard! that club of thine will float
Upon the summer floods, and not my bones.
But rise, and be not wroth! not wroth am I;
No, when I see thee, wrath forsakes my soul.

Thou say'st thou art not Rustum; be it so!
Who art thou, then, that canst so touch my soul?
Boy as I am, I have seen battles too –
Have waded foremost in their bloody waves,
And heard their hollow roar of dying men;
But never was my heart thus touched before.
Are they from heaven, these softenings of the heart?
O thou old warrior, let us yield to Heaven!
Come, plant we here in earth our angry spears,
And make a truce, and sit upon this sand,
And pledge each other in red wine, like friends,
And thou shalt talk to me of Rustum's deeds.
There are enough foes in the Persian host,
Whom I may meet, and strike, and feel no pang;
Champions enough Afrasiab has, whom thou
Mayst fight; fight *them*, when they confront thy spear!
But oh, let there be peace 'twixt thee and me!'

  He ceased, but while he spake, Rustum had risen,
And stood erect, trembling with rage; his club
He left to lie, but had regained his spear,
Whose fiery point now in his mailed right hand
Blazed bright and baleful, like that autumn star,
The baleful sign of fevers; dust had soiled
His stately crest, and dimmed his glittering arms.
His breast heaved, his lips foamed, and twice his voice
Was choked with rage; at last these words broke way:

  'Girl! nimble with thy feet, not with thy hands!
Curled minion, dancer, coiner of sweet words!
Fight, let me hear thy hateful voice no more!
Thou art not in Afrasiab's gardens now
With Tartar girls, with whom thou art wont to dance;

But on the Oxus sands, and in the dance
Of battle, and with me, who make no play
Of war; I fight it out, and hand to hand.
Speak not to me of truce, and pledge, and wine!
Remember all thy valour; try thy feints
And cunning! all the pity I had is gone,
Because thou hast shamed me before both the hosts
With thy light skipping tricks and thy girl's wiles.'

  He spoke, and Sohrab kindled at his taunts,
And he too drew his sword; at once they rushed
Together, as two eagles on one prey
Come rushing down together from the clouds,
One from the east, one from the west; their shields
Dashed with a clang together, and a din
Rose, such as that the sinewy woodcutters
Make often in the forest's heart at morn,
Of hewing axes, crashing trees – such blows
Rustum and Sohrab on each other hailed.
And you would say that sun and stars took part
In that unnatural conflict; for a cloud
Grew suddenly in heaven, and darked the sun
Over the fighters' heads; and a wind rose
Under their feet, and moaning swept the plain,
And in a sandy whirlwind wrapped the pair.
In gloom they twain were wrapped, and they alone;
For both the onlooking hosts on either hand
Stood in broad daylight, and the sky was pure,
And the sun sparkled on the Oxus stream.
But in the gloom they fought, with bloodshot eyes
And labouring breath; first Rustum struck the shield
Which Sohrab held stiff out; the steel-spiked spear

Rent the tough plates, but failed to reach the skin,
And Rustum plucked it back with angry groan.
Then Sohrab with his sword smote Rustum's helm,
Nor clove its steel quite through; but all the crest
He shore away, and that proud horsehair plume,
Never till now defiled, sank to the dust;
And Rustum bowed his head; but then the gloom
Grew blacker, thunder rumbled in the air,
And lightnings rent the cloud; and Ruksh, the horse,
Who stood at hand, uttered a dreadful cry;
No horse's cry was that, most like the roar
Of some pained desert lion, who all day
Hath trailed the hunter's javelin in his side,
And comes at night to die upon the sand.
The two hosts heard that cry, and quaked for fear,
And Oxus curdled as it crossed his stream.
But Sohrab heard, and quailed not, but rushed on,
And struck again; and again Rustum bowed
His head; but this time all the blade, like glass,
Sprang in a thousand shivers on the helm,
And in the hand the hilt remained alone.
Then Rustum raised his head; his dreadful eyes
Glared, and he shook on high his menacing spear,
And shouted: *Rustum!* Sohrab heard that shout,
And shrank amazed; back he recoiled one step,
And scanned with blinking eyes the advancing form;
And then he stood bewildered; and he dropped
His covering shield, and the spear pierced his side.
He reeled, and staggering back, sank to the ground;
And then the gloom dispersed, and the wind fell,
And the bright sun broke forth, and melted all

The cloud; and the two armies saw the pair –
Saw Rustum standing, safe upon his feet,
And Sohrab, wounded, on the bloody sand.

   Then, with a bitter smile, Rustum began:
'Sohrab, thou thoughtest in thy mind to kill
A Persian lord this day, and strip his corpse,
And bear thy trophies to Afrasiab's tent.
Or else that the great Rustum would come down
Himself to fight, and that thy wiles would move
His heart to take a gift, and let thee go.
And then that all the Tartar host would praise
Thy courage or thy craft, and spread thy fame,
To glad thy father in his weak old age.
Fool, thou art slain, and by an unknown man!
Dearer to the red jackals shalt thou be
Than to thy friends, and to thy father old.'

   And, with a fearless mien, Sohrab replied:
'Unknown thou art, yet thy fierce vaunt is vain.
Thou dost not slay me, proud and boastful man!
No! Rustum slays me, and this filial heart.
For were I matched with ten such men as thee,
And I were that which till today I was,
They should be lying here, I standing there.
But that belovèd name unnerved my arm –
That name, and something, I confess, in thee,
Which troubles all my heart, and made my shield
Fall; and thy spear transfixed an unarmed foe.
And now thou boastest, and insult'st my fate.
But hear thou this, fierce man, tremble to hear:
The mighty Rustum shall avenge my death!
My father, whom I seek through all the world,
He shall avenge my death, and punish thee!'

As when some hunter in the spring hath found
A breeding eagle sitting on her nest,
Upon the craggy isle of a hill-lake,
And pierced her with an arrow as she rose,
And followed her to find her where she fell
Far off; anon her mate comes winging back
From hunting, and a great way off descries
His huddling young left sole; at that, he checks
His pinion, and with short uneasy sweeps
Circles above his eyry, with loud screams
Chiding his mate back to her nest; but she
Lies dying, with the arrow in her side,
In some far stony gorge out of his ken,
A heap of fluttering feathers – never more
Shall the lake glass her, flying over it;
Never the black and dripping precipices
Echo her stormy scream as she sails by –
As that poor bird flies home, nor knows his loss,
So Rustum knew not his own loss, but stood
Over his dying son, and knew him not.

   But, with a cold, incredulous voice, he said:
'What prate is this of fathers and revenge?
The mighty Rustum never had a son.'

   And, with a failing voice, Sohrab replied:
'Ah, yes, he had! and that lost son am I.
Surely the news will one day reach his ear,
Reach Rustum, where he sits, and tarries long,
Somewhere, I know not where, but far from here;
And pierce him like a stab, and make him leap
To arms, and cry for vengeance upon thee.
Fierce man, bethink thee, for an only son!

What will that grief, what will that vengeance, be?
Oh, could I live till I that grief had seen!
Yet him I pity not so much, but her,
My mother, who in Ader-baijan dwells
With that old king, her father, who grows grey
With age, and rules over the valiant Koords.
Her most I pity, who no more will see
Sohrab returning from the Tartar camp,
With spoils and honour, when the war is done.
But a dark rumour will be bruited up,
From tribe to tribe, until it reach her ear;
And then will that defenceless woman learn
That Sohrab will rejoice her sight no more;
But that in battle with a nameless foe,
By the far-distant Oxus, he is slain.'

  He spoke; and as he ceased, he wept aloud,
Thinking of her he left, and his own death.
He spoke; but Rustum listened, plunged in thought.
Nor did he yet believe it was his son
Who spoke, although he called back names he knew;
For he had had sure tidings that the babe
Which was in Ader-baijan born to him
Had been a puny girl, no boy at all –
So that sad mother sent him word, for fear
Rustum should seek the boy, to train in arms.
And so he deemed that either Sohrab took,
By a false boast, the style of Rustum's son;
Or that men gave it him, to swell his fame.
So deemed he: yet he listened, plunged in thought:
And his soul set to grief, as the vast tide
Of the bright rocking Ocean sets to shore

At the full moon; tears gathered in his eyes;
For he remembered his own early youth,
And all its bounding rapture; as, at dawn,
The shepherd from his mountain lodge descries
A far, bright city, smitten by the sun,
Through many rolling clouds – so Rustum saw
His youth; saw Sohrab's mother in her bloom;
And that old king, her father, who loved well
His wandering guest, and gave him his fair child
With joy; and all the pleasant life they led,
They three, in that long-distant summertime –
The castle, and the dewy woods, and hunt
And hound, and morn on those delightful hills
In Ader-baijan. And he saw that youth,
Of age and looks to be his own dear son,
Piteous and lovely, lying on the sand,
Like some rich hyacinth which by the scythe
Of an unskilful gardener has been cut,
Mowing the garden grass-plots near its bed,
And lies, a fragrant tower of purple bloom,
On the mown, dying grass – so Sohrab lay,
Lovely in death, upon the common sand.
And Rustum gazed on him with grief, and said:

   'O Sohrab, thou indeed art such a son
Whom Rustum, wert thou his, might well have loved.
Yet here thou errest, Sohrab, or else men
Have told thee false – thou art not Rustum's son.
For Rustum had no son; one child he had –
But one – a girl; who with her mother now
Plies some light female task, nor dreams of us –
Of us she dreams not, nor of wounds, nor war.'

But Sohrab answered him in wrath; for now
The anguish of the deep-fixed spear grew fierce,
And he desired to draw forth the steel,
And let the blood flow free, and so to die —
But first he would convince his stubborn foe;
And, rising sternly on one arm, he said:

'Man, who art thou who dost deny my words?
Truth sits upon the lips of dying men,
And falsehood, while I lived, was far from mine.
I tell thee, pricked upon this arm I bear
That seal which Rustum to my mother gave,
That she might prick it on the babe she bore.'

He spoke; and all the blood left Rustum's cheeks,
And his knees tottered, and he smote his hand
Against his breast, his heavy mailèd hand,
That the hard iron corslet clanked aloud;
And to his heart he pressed the other hand,
And in a hollow voice he spake, and said:

'Sohrab, that were a proof which could not lie!
If thou show this, then art thou Rustum's son.'

Then, with weak hasty fingers, Sohrab loosed
His belt, and near the shoulder bared his arm,
And showed a sign in faint vermilion points
Pricked; as a cunning workman, in Pekin,
Pricks with vermilion some clear porcelain vase,
An emperor's gift — at early morn he paints,
And all day long, and, when night comes, the lamp
Lights up his studious forehead and thin hands —
So delicately pricked the sign appeared
On Sohrab's arm, the sign of Rustum's seal.
It was that griffin which of old reared Zal,

Rustum's great father, whom they left to die,
A helpless babe, among the mountain rocks;
Him that kind creature found, and reared, and loved –
Then Rustum took it for his glorious sign.
And Sohrab bared that image on his arm,
And himself scanned it long with mournful eyes,
And then he touched it with his hand, and said:

  'How say'st thou? Is that sign the proper sign
Of Rustum's son, or of some other man's?'

  He spoke; but Rustum gazed, and gazed, and stood
Speechless; and then he uttered one sharp cry:
O boy – thy father! – and his voice choked there.
And then a dark cloud passed before his eyes,
And his head swam, and he sank down to earth.
But Sohrab crawled to where he lay, and cast
His arms about his neck, and kissed his lips,
And with fond faltering fingers stroked his cheeks,
Trying to call him back to life; and life
Came back to Rustum, and he oped his eyes,
And they stood wide with horror; and he seized
In both his hands the dust which lay around,
And threw it on his head, and smirched his hair,
His hair, and face, and beard, and glittering arms;
And strong convulsive groanings shook his breast,
And his sobs choked him; and he clutched his sword,
To draw it, and for ever let life out.
But Sohrab saw his thought, and held his hands,
And with a soothing voice he spake, and said:

  'Father, forbear! for I but meet today
The doom which at my birth was written down
In heaven, and thou art Heaven's unconscious hand.

Surely my heart cried out that it was thou,
When first I saw thee; and thy heart spoke too,
I know it! but fate trod those promptings down
Under its iron heel; fate, fate engaged
The strife, and hurled me on my father's spear.
But let us speak no more of this! I find
My father; let me feel that I have found!
Come, sit beside me on this sand, and take
My head betwixt thy hands, and kiss my cheeks,
And wash them with thy tears, and say: *My son!*
Quick, quick! for numbered are my sands of life,
And swift; for like the lightning to this field
I came, and like the wind I go away –
Sudden, and swift, and like a passing wind.
But it was writ in heaven that this should be.'

So said he, and his voice released the heart
Of Rustum, and his tears broke forth; he cast
His arms round his son's neck, and wept aloud,
And kissed him. And awe fell on both the hosts,
When they saw Rustum's grief; and Ruksh, the horse,
With his head bowing to the ground and mane
Sweeping the dust, came near, and in mute woe
First to the one then to the other moved
His head, as if inquiring what their grief
Might mean; and from his dark, compassionate eyes,
The big warm tears rolled down, and caked the sand.
But Rustum chid him with stern voice, and said:

'Ruksh, now thou grievest; but, O Ruksh, thy feet
Should then have rotted on their nimble joints,
When first they bore thy master to this field!'

But Sohrab looked upon the horse, and said:
'Is this, then, Ruksh? How often, in past days,
My mother told me of thee, thou brave steed,
My terrible father's terrible horse! and said,
That I should one day find thy lord and thee.
Come, let me lay my hand upon thy mane!
O Ruksh, thou art more fortunate than I;
For thou hast gone where I shall never go,
And snuffed the breezes of my father's home.
And thou hast trod the sands of Seistan,
And seen the River of Helmund, and the Lake
Of Zirrah; and the aged Zal himself
Has often stroked thy neck, and given thee food,
Corn in a golden platter, soaked with wine,
And said: *O Ruksh! bear Rustum well!* – but I
Have never known my grandsire's furrowed face,
Nor seen his lofty house in Seistan,
Nor slaked my thirst at the clear Helmund stream;
But lodged among my father's foes, and seen
Afrasiab's cities only, Samarcand,
Bokhara, and lone Khiva in the waste,
And the black Toorkmun tents; and only drunk
The desert rivers, Moorghab and Tejend,
Kohik, and where the Kalmuks feed their sheep,
The northern Sir; and this great Oxus stream,
The yellow Oxus, by whose brink I die.'

Then, with a heavy groan, Rustum bewailed:
'Oh, that its waves were flowing over me!
Oh, that I saw its grains of yellow silt
Roll tumbling in the current o'er my head!'

But, with a grave mild voice, Sohrab replied:
'Desire not that, my father! thou must live.
For some are born to do great deeds, and live
As some are born to be obscured, and die.
Do thou the deeds I die too young to do,
And reap a second glory in thine age;
Thou art my father, and thy gain is mine.
But come! thou seest this great host of men
Which follow me; I pray thee, slay not these!
Let me entreat for them; what have they done?
They followed me, my hope, my fame, my star.
Let them all cross the Oxus back in peace.
But me thou must bear hence, not send with them,
But carry me with thee to Seistan,
And place me on a bed, and mourn for me,
Thou, and the snow-haired Zal, and all thy friends.
And thou must lay me in that lovely earth,
And heap a stately mound above my bones,
And plant a far-seen pillar over all.
That so the passing horseman on the waste
May see my tomb a great way off, and cry:
Sohrab, the mighty Rustum's son, lies there,
Whom his great father did in ignorance kill!
And I be not forgotten in my grave.'

  And, with a mournful voice, Rustum replied:
'Fear not! as thou hast said, Sohrab my son,
So shall it be; for I will burn my tents,
And quit the host, and bear thee hence with me,
And carry thee away to Seistan,
And place thee on a bed, and mourn for thee,
With the snow-headed Zal, and all my friends.

And I will lay thee in that lovely earth,
And heap a stately mound above thy bones,
And plant a far-seen pillar over all,
And men shall not forget thee in thy grave.
And I will spare thy host; yea, let them go!
Let them all cross the Oxus back in peace!
What should I do with slaying any more?
For would that all whom I have ever slain
Might be once more alive; my bitterest foes,
And they who were called champions in their time,
And through whose death I won that fame I have —
And I were nothing but a common man,
A poor, mean soldier, and without renown,
So thou mightest live too, my son, my son!
Or rather would that I, even I myself,
Might now be lying on this bloody sand,
Near death, and by an ignorant stroke of thine,
Not thou of mine! and I might die, not thou;
And I, not thou, be borne to Seistan;
And Zal might weep above my grave, not thine;
And say: *O son, I weep thee not too sore,*
For willingly, I know, thou met'st thine end!
But now in blood and battles was my youth,
And full of blood and battles is my age,
And I shall never end this life of blood.'

   Then, at the point of death, Sohrab replied:
'A life of blood indeed, thou dreadful man!
But thou shalt yet have peace; only not now,
Not yet! but thou shalt have it on that day,
When thou shalt sail in a high-masted ship,
Thou and the other peers of Kai Khosroo,

Returning home over the salt blue sea,
From laying thy dear master in his grave.'

   And Rustum gazed in Sohrab's face, and said:
'Soon be that day, my son, and deep that sea!
Till then, if fate so wills, let me endure.'

   He spoke; and Sohrab smiled on him, and took
The spear, and drew it from his side, and eased
His wound's imperious anguish; but the blood
Came welling from the open gash, and life
Flowed with the stream; all down his cold white side
The crimson torrent ran, dim now and soiled,
Like the soiled tissue of white violets
Left, freshly gathered, on their native bank,
By children whom their nurses call with haste
Indoors from the sun's eye; his head drooped low,
His limbs grew slack; motionless, white, he lay –
White, with eyes closed; only when heavy gasps,
Deep heavy gasps quivering through all his frame,
Convulsed him back to life, he opened them,
And fixed them feebly on his father's face;
Till now all strength was ebbed, and from his limbs
Unwillingly the spirit fled away,
Regretting the warm mansion which it left,
And youth, and bloom, and this delightful world.

   So, on the bloody sand, Sohrab lay dead;
And the great Rustum drew his horseman's cloak
Down o'er his face, and sat by his dead son.
As those black granite pillars, once high-reared
By Jemshid in Persepolis, to bear
His house, now 'mid their broken flights of steps
Lie prone, enormous, down the mountainside –
So in the sand lay Rustum by his son.

And night came down over the solemn waste,
And the two gazing hosts, and that sole pair,
And darkened all; and a cold fog, with night,
Crept from the Oxus. Soon a hum arose,
As of a great assembly loosed, and fires
Began to twinkle through the fog; for now
Both armies moved to camp, and took their meal;
The Persians took it on the open sands
Southward, the Tartars by the river marge;
And Rustum and his son were left alone.

But the majestic river floated on,
Out of the mist and hum of that low land,
Into the frosty starlight, and there moved,
Rejoicing, through the hushed Chorasmian waste,
Under the solitary moon; he flowed
Right for the polar star, past Orgunjè,
Brimming, and bright, and large; then sands begin
To hem his watery march, and dam his streams,
And split his currents; that for many a league
The shorn and parcelled Oxus strains along
Through beds of sand and matted rushy isles –
Oxus, forgetting the bright speed he had
In his high mountain cradle in Pamere,
A foiled circuitous wanderer – till at last
The longed-for dash of waves is heard, and wide
His luminous home of waters opens, bright
And tranquil, from whose floor the new-bathed stars
Emerge, and shine upon the Aral Sea.

1852–53

The Scholar-Gipsy

Go, for they call you, shepherd, from the hill;
   Go, shepherd, and untie the wattled cotes!
     No longer leave thy wistful flock unfed,
   Nor let thy bawling fellows rack their throats,
     Nor the cropped herbage shoot another head.
       But when the fields are still,
  And the tired men and dogs all gone to rest,
    And only the white sheep are sometimes seen
    Cross and recross the strips of moon-blanched green,
Come, shepherd, and again begin the quest!

Here, where the reaper was at work of late —
   In this high field's dark corner, where he leaves
     His coat, his basket and his earthen cruse,
   And in the sun all morning binds the sheaves,
     Then here at noon comes back his stores to use —
       Here will I sit and wait,
  While to my ear from uplands far away
    The bleating of the folded flocks is borne,
    With distant cries of reapers in the corn —
All the live murmur of a summer's day.

Screened is this nook o'er the high, half-reaped field,
   And here till sundown, shepherd! will I be.
     Through the thick corn the scarlet poppies peep,
   And round green roots and yellowing stalks I see
     Pale pink convolvulus in tendrils creep;
       And air-swept lindens yield

Their scent, and rustle down their perfumed showers
  Of bloom on the bent grass where I am laid,
  And bower me from the August sun with shade;
And the eye travels down to Oxford's towers.

And near me on the grass lies Glanvil's book –
  Come, let me read the oft-read tale again!
    The story of that Oxford scholar poor,
  Of pregnant parts and quick inventive brain,
    Who, tired of knocking at preferment's door,
      One summer morn forsook
  His friends, and went to learn the Gipsy lore,
    And roamed the world with that wild brotherhood,
    And came, as most men deemed, to little good,
  But came to Oxford and his friends no more.

But once, years after, in the country lanes,
  Two scholars, whom at college erst he knew,
    Met him, and of his way of life enquired;
  Whereat he answered that the Gipsy crew,
    His mates, had arts to rule as they desired
      The workings of men's brains,
  And they can bind them to what thoughts they will.
    'And I,' he said, 'the secret of their art,
    When fully learned, will to the world impart;
  But it needs heaven-sent moments for this skill.'

This said, he left them, and returned no more.
  But rumours hung about the countryside,
    That the lost Scholar long was seen to stray,
  Seen by rare glimpses, pensive and tongue-tied,

In hat of antique shape, and cloak of grey,
   The same the Gipsies wore.
Shepherds had met him on the Hurst in spring;
   At some lone alehouse in the Berkshire moors,
      On the warm ingle-bench, the smock-frocked boors
Had found him seated at their entering,

But, 'mid their drink and clatter, he would fly.
   And I myself seem half to know thy looks,
      And put the shepherds, wanderer! on thy trace;
      And boys who in lone wheatfields scare the rooks
         I ask if thou hast passed their quiet place;
            Or in my boat I lie
      Moored to the cool bank in the summer heats,
         'Mid wide grass meadows which the sunshine fills,
         And watch the warm, green-muffled Cumner hills,
      And wonder if thou haunt'st their shy retreats.

For most, I know, thou lov'st retired ground!
   Thee at the ferry Oxford riders blithe,
      Returning home on summer nights, have met
   Crossing the stripling Thames at Bablock Hythe,
      Trailing in the cool stream thy fingers wet,
         As the punt's rope chops round;
      And leaning backward in a pensive dream,
         And fostering in thy lap a heap of flowers
         Plucked in shy fields and distant Wychwood bowers,
      And thine eyes resting on the moonlit stream.

And then they land, and thou art seen no more!
   Maidens, who from the distant hamlets come
      To dance around the Fyfield elm in May,

Oft through the darkening fields have seen thee roam,
    Or cross a stile into the public way.
       Oft thou hast given them store
Of flowers – the frail-leafed, white anemone,
    Dark bluebells drenched with dews of summer eves,
    And purple orchises with spotted leaves –
But none hath words she can report of thee.

And, above Godstow Bridge, when haytime's here
    In June, and many a scythe in sunshine flames,
       Men who through those wide fields of breezy grass,
Where black-winged swallows haunt the glittering Thames,
    To bathe in the abandoned lasher pass,
       Have often passed thee near
Sitting upon the riverbank o'ergrown;
    Marked thine outlandish garb, thy figure spare,
    Thy dark vague eyes, and soft abstracted air –
But, when they came from bathing, thou wast gone!

At some lone homestead in the Cumner hills,
    Where at her open door the housewife darns,
       Thou hast been seen, or hanging on a gate
To watch the threshers in the mossy barns.
    Children, who early range these slopes and late
       For cresses from the rills,
Have known thee eying, all an April day,
    The springing pastures and the feeding kine;
    And marked thee, when the stars come out and shine,
Through the long dewy grass move slow away.

In autumn, on the skirts of Bagley Wood –
   Where most the Gipsies by the turf-edged way
      Pitch their smoked tents, and every bush you see
   With scarlet patches tagged and shreds of grey,
      Above the forest ground called Thessaly –
         The blackbird picking food
   Sees thee, nor stops his meal, nor fears at all;
      So often has he known thee past him stray,
      Rapt, twirling in thy hand a withered spray,
   And waiting for the spark from heaven to fall.

And once, in winter, on the causeway chill
   Where home through flooded fields foot-travellers go,
      Have I not passed thee on the wooden bridge
   Wrapped in thy cloak and battling with the snow,
      Thy face toward Hinksey and its wintry ridge?
         And thou hast climbed the hill,
   And gained the white brow of the Cumner range;
      Turned once to watch, while thick the snowflakes fall,
      The line of festal light in Christ Church Hall –
   Then sought thy straw in some sequestered grange.

But what – I dream! Two hundred years are flown
   Since first thy story ran through Oxford halls,
      And the grave Glanvil did the tale inscribe
   That thou wert wandered from the studious walls
      To learn strange arts, and join a Gipsy tribe;
         And thou from earth art gone
   Long since, and in some quiet churchyard laid –
      Some country nook, where o'er thy unknown grave
      Tall grasses and white flowering nettles wave,
   Under a dark, red-fruited yew tree's shade.

– No, no, thou hast not felt the lapse of hours!
   For what wears out the life of mortal men?
      'Tis that from change to change their being rolls;
   'Tis that repeated shocks, again, again,
      Exhaust the energy of strongest souls,
         And numb the elastic powers,
   Till having used our nerves with bliss and teen,
      And tired upon a thousand schemes our wit,
      To the just-pausing Genius we remit
Our worn-out life, and are – what we have been.

Thou hast not lived, why shouldst thou perish, so?
   Thou hadst *one* aim, *one* business, *one* desire;
      Else wert thou long since numbered with the dead!
   Else hadst thou spent, like other men, thy fire!
      The generations of thy peers are fled,
         And we ourselves shall go;
   But thou possessest an immortal lot,
      And we imagine thee exempt from age,
      And living as thou liv'st on Glanvil's page,
Because thou hadst – what we, alas! have not.

For early didst thou leave the world, with powers
   Fresh, undiverted to the world without,
      Firm to their mark, not spent on other things;
   Free from the sick fatigue, the languid doubt,
      Which much to have tried, in much been baffled, brings.
         O life unlike to ours!
   Who fluctuate idly without term or scope,
      Of whom each strives, nor knows for what he strives,
      And each half-lives a hundred different lives;
   Who wait like thee, but not, like thee, in hope.

Thou waitest for the spark from heaven! and we,
　　Light half-believers of our casual creeds,
　　　　Who never deeply felt, nor clearly willed,
　　Whose insight never has borne fruit in deeds,
　　　　Whose vague resolves never have been fulfilled;
　　　　　　For whom each year we see
　　Breeds new beginnings, disappointments new;
　　　　Who hesitate and falter life away,
　　　　And lose tomorrow the ground won today –
　　Ah! do not we, wanderer! await it too?

Yes, we await it! – but it still delays,
　　And then we suffer! and amongst us one,
　　　　Who most has suffered, takes dejectedly
　　His seat upon the intellectual throne;
　　　　And all his store of sad experience he
　　　　　　Lays bare of wretched days;
　　Tells us his misery's birth and growth and signs,
　　　　And how the dying spark of hope was fed,
　　　　And how the breast was soothed, and how the head,
　　And all his hourly varied anodynes.

This for our wisest! and we others pine,
　　And wish the long unhappy dream would end,
　　　　And waive all claim to bliss, and try to bear;
　　With close-lipped patience for our only friend,
　　　　Sad patience, too near neighbour to despair –
　　　　　　But none has hope like thine!
　　Thou through the fields and through the woods dost stray,
　　　　Roaming the countryside, a truant boy,
　　　　Nursing thy project in unclouded joy,
　　And every doubt long blown by time away.

O born in days when wits were fresh and clear,
    And life ran gaily as the sparkling Thames;
        Before this strange disease of modern life,
    With its sick hurry, its divided aims,
        Its heads o'ertaxed, its palsied hearts, was rife –
            Fly hence, our contact fear!
    Still fly, plunge deeper in the bowering wood!
        Averse, as Dido did with gesture stern
        From her false friend's approach in Hades turn,
    Wave us away, and keep thy solitude!

Still nursing the unconquerable hope,
    Still clutching the inviolable shade,
        With a free, onward impulse brushing through,
    By night, the silvered branches of the glade –
        Far on the forest skirts, where none pursue,
            On some mild pastoral slope
    Emerge, and resting on the moonlit pales
        Freshen thy flowers as in former years
        With dew, or listen with enchanted ears,
    From the dark dingles, to the nightingales!

But fly our paths, our feverish contact fly!
    For strong the infection of our mental strife,
        Which, though it gives no bliss, yet spoils for rest;
    And we should win thee from thy own fair life,
        Like us distracted, and like us unblest.
            Soon, soon thy cheer would die,
    Thy hopes grow timorous, and unfixed thy powers,
        And thy clear aims be cross and shifting made;
        And then thy glad perennial youth would fade,
    Fade, and grow old at last, and die like ours.

Then fly our greetings, fly our speech and smiles!
   – As some grave Tyrian trader, from the sea,
     Descried at sunrise an emerging prow
  Lifting the cool-haired creepers stealthily,
     The fringes of a southward-facing brow
        Among the Aegean isles;
 And saw the merry Grecian coaster come,
     Freighted with amber grapes, and Chian wine,
     Green, bursting figs, and tunnies steeped in brine –
And knew the intruders on his ancient home,

The young light-hearted masters of the waves –
    And snatched his rudder, and shook out more sail,
    And day and night held on indignantly
  O'er the blue Midland waters with the gale,
     Betwixt the Syrtes and soft Sicily,
        To where the Atlantic raves
  Outside the western straits; and unbent sails
     There where down cloudy cliffs, through sheets of foam,
     Shy traffickers, the dark Iberians come;
And on the beach undid his corded bales.

1852–53

Requiescat

Strew on her roses, roses,
   And never a spray of yew!
In quiet she reposes;
   Ah, would that I did too!

Her mirth the world required;
   She bathed it in smiles of glee.
But her heart was tired, tired,
   And now they let her be.

Her life was turning, turning,
   In mazes of heat and sound.
But for peace her soul was yearning,
   And now peace laps her round.

Her cabined, ample spirit,
   It fluttered and failed for breath.
Tonight it doth inherit
   The vasty hall of death.

(?) 1849–53

from *Balder Dead*

Forth from the east, up the ascent of heaven,
Day drove his courser with the shining mane;
And in Valhalla, from his gable perch,
The golden-crested cock began to crow.
Hereafter, in the blackest dead of night,
With shrill and dismal cries that bird shall crow,
Warning the Gods that foes draw nigh to heaven;
But now he crew at dawn, a cheerful note,
To wake the Gods and Heroes to their tasks.
And all the Gods and all the Heroes woke.
And from their beds the Heroes rose, and donned
Their arms, and led their horses from the stall,
And mounted them, and in Valhalla's court
Were ranged; and then the daily fray began.
And all day long they there are hacked and hewn
'Mid dust, and groans, and limbs lopped off, and blood;
But all at night return to Odin's hall,
Woundless and fresh: such lot is theirs in heaven.
And the Valkyries on their steeds went forth
Toward Earth and fights of men; and at their side
Skulda, the youngest of the Nornies, rode;
And over Bifrost, where is Heimdall's watch,
Past Midgard fortress, down to Earth they came;
There through some battlefield, where men fall fast,
Their horses fetlock-deep in blood, they ride,
And pick the bravest warriors out for death,
Whom they bring back with them at night to heaven,
To glad the gods, and feast in Odin's hall.

Book II (1853–54)

Haworth Churchyard

APRIL, 1855

Where, under Loughrigg, the stream
Of Rotha sparkles through fields
Vested for ever with green,
Four years since, in the house
Of a gentle spirit, now dead –
Wordsworth's son-in-law, friend –
I saw the meeting of two
Gifted women. The one,
Brilliant with recent renown,
Young, unpractised, had told
With a master's accent her feigned
Story of passionate life;
The other, maturer in fame,
Earning, she too, her praise
First in fiction, had since
Widened her sweep, and surveyed
History, politics, mind.

The two held converse; they wrote
In a book which of world-famous souls
Kept the memorial: bard,
Warrior, statesman, had signed
Their names; chief glory of all,
Scott had bestowed there his last
Breathings of song, with a pen
Tottering, a death-stricken hand.

Hope at that meeting smiled fair.
Years in number, it seemed,
Lay before both, and a fame
Heightened, and multiplied power.
Behold! The elder, today,
Lies expecting from death,
In mortal weakness, a last
Summons! the younger is dead!

First to the living we pay
Mournful homage; the Muse
Gains not an earth-deafened ear.

Hail to the steadfast soul,
Which, unflinching and keen,
Wrought to erase from its depth
Mist and illusion and fear!
Hail to the spirit which dared
Trust its own thoughts, before yet
Echoed her back by the crowd!
Hail to the courage which gave
Voice to its creed, ere the creed
Won consecration from time!

Turn we next to the dead.
– How shall we honour the young,
The ardent, the gifted? how mourn?
Console we cannot, her ear
Is deaf. Far northward from here,
In a churchyard high 'mid the moors
Of Yorkshire, a little earth
Stops it for ever to praise.

Where, behind Keighley, the road
Up to the heart of the moors
Between heath-clad showery hills
Runs, and colliers' carts
Poach the deep ways coming down,
And a rough, grimed race have their homes –
There on its slope is built
The moorland town. But the church
Stands on the crest of the hill,
Lonely and bleak; at its side
The parsonage house and the graves.

Strew with laurel the grave
Of the early-dying! Alas,
Early she goes on the path
To the silent country, and leaves
Half her laurels unwon,
Dying too soon! – yet green
Laurels she had, and a course
Short, but redoubled by fame.

And not friendless, and not
Only with strangers to meet,
Faces ungreeting and cold,
Thou, O mourned one, today
Enterest the house of the grave!
Those of thy blood, whom thou lov'dst,
Have preceded thee – young,
Loving, a sisterly band;
Some in art, some in gift
Inferior – all in fame.
They, like friends, shall receive

This comer, greet her with joy;
Welcome the sister, the friend;
Hear with delight of thy fame!

Round thee they lie — the grass
Blows from their graves to thy own!
She whose genius, though not
Puissant like thine, was yet
Sweet and graceful; and she
(How shall I sing her?) whose soul
Knew no fellow for might,
Passion, vehemence, grief,
Daring, since Byron died,
That world-famed son of fire — she, who sank
Baffled, unknown, self-consumed;
Whose too bold dying song
Shook, like a clarion blast, my soul.

Of one, too, I have heard,
A brother — sleeps he here?
Of all that gifted race
Not the least gifted; young,
Unhappy, eloquent — the child
Of many hopes, of many tears.
O boy, if here thou sleep'st, sleep well!
On thee too did the Muse
Bright in thy cradle smile;
But some dark shadow came
(I know not what) and interposed.

Sleep, O cluster of friends,
Sleep! — or only when May,

Brought by the west wind, returns
Back to your native heaths,
And the plover is heard on the moors,
Yearly awake to behold
The opening summer, the sky,
The shining moorland — to hear
The drowsy bee, as of old,
Hum o'er the thyme, the grouse
Call from the heather in bloom!
Sleep, or only for this
Break your united repose!

EPILOGUE

So I sang; but the Muse,
Shaking her head, took the harp —
Stern interrupted my strain,
Angrily smote on the chords.

April showers
Rush o'er the Yorkshire moors.
Stormy, through driving mist,
Loom the blurred hills; the rain
Lashes the newly made grave.

Unquiet souls!
— In the dark fermentation of earth,
In the never-idle workshop of nature,
In the eternal movement,
Ye shall find yourselves again!

1855

Rugby Chapel

NOVEMBER, 1857

Coldly, sadly descends
The autumn evening. The field
Strewn with its dank yellow drifts
Of withered leaves, and the elms,
Fade into dimness apace,
Silent; hardly a shout
From a few boys late at their play!
The lights come out in the street,
In the schoolroom windows; but cold,
Solemn, unlighted, austere,
Through the gathering darkness, arise
The chapel walls, in whose bound
Thou, my father! art laid.

There thou dost lie, in the gloom
Of the autumn evening. But ah!
That word, *gloom*, to my mind
Brings thee back in the light
Of thy radiant vigour again;
In the gloom of November we passed
Days not dark at thy side;
Seasons impaired not the ray
Of thy buoyant cheerfulness clear.
Such thou wast! and I stand
In the autumn evening, and think
Of bygone autumns with thee.

Fifteen years have gone round
Since thou arosest to tread,
In the summer morning, the road
Of death, at a call unforeseen,
Sudden. For fifteen years,
We who till then in thy shade
Rested as under the boughs
Of a mighty oak, have endured
Sunshine and rain as we might,
Bare, unshaded, alone,
Lacking the shelter of thee.

O strong soul, by what shore
Tarriest thou now? For that force,
Surely, has not been left vain!
Somewhere, surely, afar,
In the sounding labour house vast
Of being, is practised that strength,
Zealous, beneficent, firm!

Yes, in some far-shining sphere,
Conscious or not of the past,
Still thou performest the word
Of the Spirit in whom thou dost live –
Prompt, unwearied, as here.
Still thou upraisest with zeal
The humble good from the ground,
Sternly repressest the bad!
Still, like a trumpet, dost rouse
Those who with half-open eyes
Tread the borderland dim

'Twixt vice and virtue; reviv'st,
Succourest! — this was thy work,
This was thy life upon Earth.

What is the course of the life
Of mortal men on the Earth?
Most men eddy about
Here and there — eat and drink,
Chatter and love and hate,
Gather and squander, are raised
Aloft, are hurled in the dust,
Striving blindly, achieving
Nothing; and then they die —
Perish; and no one asks
Who or what they have been,
More than he asks what waves,
In the moonlit solitudes mild
Of the midmost Ocean, have swelled,
Foamed for a moment, and gone.

And there are some whom a thirst
Ardent, unquenchable, fires,
Not with the crowd to be spent,
Not without aim to go round
In an eddy of purposeless dust,
Effort unmeaning and vain.
Ah yes! some of us strive
Not without action to die
Fruitless, but something to snatch
From dull oblivion, nor all
Glut the devouring grave.

We, we have chosen our path —
Path to a clear-purposed goal,
Path of advance! — but it leads
A long, steep journey, through sunk
Gorges, o'er mountains in snow.
Cheerful, with friends, we set forth —
Then, on the height, comes the storm.
Thunder crashes from rock
To rock, the cataracts reply,
Lightnings dazzle our eyes.
Roaring torrents have breached
The track, the stream-bed descends
In the place where the wayfarer once
Planted his footstep — the spray
Boils o'er its borders! aloft,
The unseen snowbeds dislodge
Their hanging ruin; alas,
Havoc is made in our train!
Friends, who set forth at our side,
Falter, are lost in the storm.
We, we only are left!
With frowning foreheads, with lips
Sternly compressed, we strain on,
On — and at nightfall at last
Come to the end of our way,
To the lonely inn 'mid the rocks;
Where the gaunt and taciturn host
Stands on the threshold, the wind
Shaking his thin white hairs —
Holds his lantern to scan
Our storm-beat figures, and asks:

Whom in our party we bring?
Whom we have left in the snow?

Sadly we answer: We bring
Only ourselves! we lost
Sight of the rest in the storm.
Hardly ourselves we fought through,
Stripped, without friends, as we are.
Friends, companions and train,
The avalanche swept from our side.

But thou wouldst not *alone*
Be saved, my father! *alone*
Conquer and come to thy goal,
Leaving the rest in the wild.
We were weary, and we
Fearful, and we in our march
Fain to drop down and to die.
Still thou turnedst, and still
Beckonedst the trembler, and still
Gavest the weary thy hand.

If, in the paths of the world,
Stones might have wounded thy feet,
Toil or dejection have tried
Thy spirit, of that we saw
Nothing – to us thou wast still
Cheerful, and helpful, and firm!
Therefore to thee it was given
Many to save with thyself;
And, at the end of thy day,

O faithful shepherd! to come,
Bringing thy sheep in thy hand.

And through thee I believe
In the noble and great who are gone;
Pure souls honoured and blest
By former ages, who else –
Such, so soulless, so poor,
Is the race of men whom I see –
Seemed but a dream of the heart,
Seemed but a cry of desire.
Yes! I believe that there lived
Others like thee in the past,
Not like the men of the crowd
Who all round me today
Bluster or cringe, and make life
Hideous and arid and vile;
But souls tempered with fire,
Fervent, heroic and good,
Helpers and friends of mankind.

Servants of God!– or sons
Shall I not call you? because
Not as servants ye knew
Your Father's innermost mind,
His who unwillingly sees
One of his little ones lost –
Yours is the praise, if mankind
Hath not as yet in its march
Fainted and fallen and died.

See! In the rocks of the world
Marches the host of mankind,
A feeble, wavering line.
Where are they tending? – A God
Marshalled them, gave them their goal.
Ah, but the way is so long!
Years they have been in the wild!
Sore thirst plagues them, the rocks,
Rising all round, overawe;
Factions divide them, their host
Threatens to break, to dissolve.
– Ah, keep, keep them combined!
Else, of the myriads who fill
That army, not one shall arrive;
Sole they shall stray; in the rocks
Stagger for ever in vain,
Die one by one in the waste.

Then, in such hour of need
Of your fainting, dispirited race,
Ye, like angels appear,
Radiant with ardour divine!
Beacons of hope, ye appear!
Languor is not in your heart,
Weakness is not in your word,
Weariness not on your brow.
Ye alight in our van! at your voice,
Panic, despair, flee away.
Ye move through the ranks, recall
The stragglers, refresh the outworn,
Praise, re-inspire the brave!

Order, courage, return.
Eyes rekindling, and prayers,
Follow your steps as ye go.
Ye fill up the gaps in our files,
Strengthen the wavering line,
Stablish, continue our march,
On, to the bound of the waste,
On, to the City of God.

1857–60

Stanzas from Carnac

Far on its rocky knoll descried,
Saint Michael's chapel cuts the sky.
I climbed; beneath me, bright and wide,
Lay the lone coast of Brittany.

Bright in the sunset, weird and still,
It lay beside the Atlantic wave,
As though the wizard Merlin's will
Yet charmed it from his forest grave.

Behind me on their grassy sweep,
Bearded with lichen, scrawled and grey,
The giant stones of Carnac sleep,
In the mild evening of the May.

No priestly stern procession now
Moves through their rows of pillars old;
No victims bleed, no Druids bow –
Sheep make the daisied aisles their fold.

From bush to bush the cuckoo flies,
The orchis red gleams everywhere;
Gold furze with broom in blossom vies,
The bluebells perfume all the air.

And o'er the glistening, lonely land,
Rise up, all round, the Christian spires;
The church of Carnac, by the strand,
Catches the westering sun's last fires.

And there, across the watery way,
See, low above the tide at flood,
The sickle-sweep of Quiberon Bay,
Whose beach once ran with loyal blood!

And beyond that, the Atlantic wide.
All round, no soul, no boat, no hail;
But, on the horizon's verge descried,
Hangs, touched with light, one snowy sail.

Ah! where is he who should have come
Where that far sail is passing now,
Past the Loire's mouth, and by the foam
Of Finistère's unquiet brow,

Home, round into the English wave?
– He tarries where the Rock of Spain
Mediterranean waters lave;
He enters not the Atlantic main.

Oh, could he once have reached this air
Freshened by plunging tides, by showers,
Have felt this breath he loved, of fair
Cool northern fields, and grass, and flowers!

He longed for it – pressed on. In vain!
At the Straits failed that spirit brave.
The south was parent of his pain,
The south is mistress of his grave.

1859

Rachel

I

In Paris all looked hot and like to fade;
Sere, in the garden of the Tuileries,
Sere with September, drooped the chestnut trees;
'Twas dawn, a brougham rolled through the streets, and made

Halt at the white and silent colonnade
Of the French Theatre. Worn with disease,
Rachel, with eyes no gazing can appease,
Sat in the brougham and those blank walls surveyed.

She follows the gay world, whose swarms have fled
To Switzerland, to Baden, to the Rhine;
Why stops she by this empty playhouse drear?

Ah, where the spirit its highest life hath led,
All spots, matched with that spot, are less divine;
And Rachel's Switzerland, her Rhine, is here!

II

Unto a lonely villa, in a dell
Above the fragrant warm Provençal shore,
The dying Rachel in a chair they bore
Up the steep pine-plumed paths of the Estrelle,

And laid her in a stately room, where fell
The shadow of a marble Muse of yore,

The rose-crowned queen of legendary lore,
Polymnia, full on her deathbed. 'Twas well!

The fret and misery of our northern towns,
In this her life's last day, our poor, our pain,
Our jangle of false wits, our climate's frowns,

Do for this radiant Greek-souled artist cease;
Sole object of her dying eyes remain
The beauty and the glorious art of Greece.

III

Sprung from the blood of Israel's scattered race,
At a mean inn in German Aarau born,
To forms from antique Greece and Rome uptorn,
Tricked out with a Parisian speech and face,

Imparting life renewed, old classic grace;
Then soothing with thy Christian strain forlorn,
À Kempis! her departing soul outworn,
While by her bedside Hebrew rites have place –

Ah, not the radiant spirit of Greece alone
She had – one power, which made her breast its home!
In her, like us, there clashed contending powers,

Germany, France, Christ, Moses, Athens, Rome.
The strife, the mixture in her soul, are ours;
Her genius and her glory are her own.

1863

West London

Crouched on the pavement, close by Belgrave Square,
A tramp I saw, ill, moody and tongue-tied;
A babe was in her arms, and at her side
A girl; their clothes were rags, their feet were bare.

Some labouring men, whose work lay somewhere there,
Passed opposite; she touched her girl, who hied
Across, and begged, and came back satisfied.
The rich she had let pass with frozen stare.

Thought I: 'Above her state this spirit towers;
She will not ask of aliens, but of friends,
Of sharers in a common human fate.

She turns from that cold succour, which attends
The unknown little from the unknowing great,
And points us to a better time than ours.'

(?) 1863

Worldly Place

Even in a palace, life may be led well!
So spake the imperial sage, purest of men,
Marcus Aurelius. But the stifling den
Of common life, where, crowded up pell-mell,

Our freedom for a little bread we sell,
And drudge under some foolish master's ken
Who rates us if we peer outside our pen —
Matched with a palace, is not this a hell?

Even in a palace! On his truth sincere,
Who spoke these words, no shadow ever came;
And when my ill-schooled spirit is aflame

Some nobler, ampler stage of life to win,
I'll stop, and say: 'There were no succour here!
The aids to noble life are all within.'

1863

Thyrsis

A MONODY *to commemorate the author's friend,*
ARTHUR HUGH CLOUGH, *who died at Florence,* 1861.

How changed is here each spot man makes or fills!
   In the two Hinkseys nothing keeps the same;
      The village street its haunted mansion lacks,
   And from the sign is gone Sibylla's name,
      And from the roofs the twisted chimney stacks –
         Are ye too changed, ye hills?
See, 'tis no foot of unfamiliar men
   Tonight from Oxford up your pathway strays!
   Here came I often, often, in old days –
Thyrsis and I: we still had Thyrsis then.

Runs it not here, the track by Childsworth Farm,
   Past the high wood, to where the elm tree crowns
      The hill behind whose ridge the sunset flames?
   The signal-elm, that looks on Ilsley Downs,
      The Vale, the three lone weirs, the youthful Thames?
         This winter eve is warm;
Humid the air! leafless, yet soft as spring,
   The tender purple spray on copse and briers!
   And that sweet city with her dreaming spires,
She needs not June for beauty's heightening,

Lovely all times she lies, lovely tonight –
   Only, methinks, some loss of habit's power
      Befalls me wandering through this upland dim.

Once passed I blindfold here, at any hour;
  Now seldom come I, since I came with him.
    That single elm tree bright
Against the west – I miss it! is it gone?
  We prized it dearly; while it stood, we said,
  Our friend the Gipsy-Scholar was not dead;
While the tree lived, he in these fields lived on.

Too rare, too rare, grow now my visits here,
  But once I knew each field, each flower, each stick;
    And with the country folk acquaintance made
By barn in threshing time, by new-built rick.
  Here, too, our shepherd pipes we first assayed.
    Ah me! this many a year
My pipe is lost, my shepherd's holiday!
  Needs must I lose them, needs with heavy heart
  Into the world and wave of men depart;
But Thyrsis of his own will went away.

It irked him to be here; he could not rest.
  He loved each simple joy the country yields,
    He loved his mates; but yet he could not keep,
For that a shadow loured on the fields,
  Here with the shepherds and the silly sheep.
    Some life of men unblest
He knew, which made him droop, and filled his head.
  He went; his piping took a troubled sound
  Of storms that rage outside our happy ground;
He could not wait their passing, he is dead.

So, some tempestuous morn in early June,
    When the year's primal burst of bloom is o'er,
        Before the roses and the longest day –
    When garden walks, and all the grassy floor,
        With blossoms red and white of fallen May,
            And chestnut flowers are strewn –
So have I heard the cuckoo's parting cry,
    From the wet field, through the vexed garden trees,
    Come with the volleying rain and tossing breeze:
The bloom is gone, and with the bloom go I!

Too quick despairer, wherefore wilt thou go?
    Soon will the high Midsummer pomps come on,
        Soon will the musk carnations break and swell,
    Soon shall we have gold-dusted snapdragon,
        Sweet William with his homely cottage smell,
            And stocks in fragrant blow;
Roses that down the alleys shine afar,
    And open, jasmine-muffled lattices,
    And groups under the dreaming garden trees,
And the full moon, and the white evening star.

He hearkens not! light comer, he is flown!
    What matters it? next year he will return,
        And we shall have him in the sweet spring days,
    With whitening hedges, and uncrumpling fern,
        And bluebells trembling by the forest ways,
            And scent of hay new-mown.
But Thyrsis never more we swains shall see;
    See him come back, and cut a smoother reed,
    And blow a strain the world at last shall heed –
For Time, not Corydon, hath conquered thee!

Alack, for Corydon no rival now!
   But when Sicilian shepherds lost a mate,
      Some good survivor with his flute would go,
   Piping a ditty sad for Bion's fate;
      And cross the unpermitted ferry's flow,
         And relax Pluto's brow,
   And make leap up with joy the beauteous head
      Of Proserpine, among whose crownèd hair
      Are flowers first opened on Sicilian air,
   And flute his friend, like Orpheus, from the dead.

O easy access to the hearer's grace
   When Dorian shepherds sang to Proserpine!
      For she herself had trod Sicilian fields,
   She knew the Dorian water's gush divine,
      She knew each lily white which Enna yields,
         Each rose with blushing face;
   She loved the Dorian pipe, the Dorian strain.
      But ah, of our poor Thames she never heard!
      Her foot the Cumner cowslips never stirred;
   And we should tease her with our plaint in vain.

Well! wind-dispersed and vain the words will be,
   Yet, Thyrsis, let me give my grief its hour
      In the old haunt, and find our tree-topped hill!
   Who, if not I, for questing here hath power?
      I know the wood which hides the daffodil,
         I know the Fyfield tree,
   I know what white, what purple fritillaries
      The grassy harvest of the river fields,
      Above by Ensham, down by Sandford, yields;
   And what sedged brooks are Thames's tributaries;

I know these slopes; who knows them if not I?
    But many a dingle on the loved hill-side,
        With thorns once studded, old white-blossomed trees,
    Where thick the cowslips grew, and far descried
        High towered the spikes of purple orchises,
            Hath since our day put by
The coronals of that forgotten time;
    Down each green bank hath gone the ploughboy's team,
    And only in the hidden brookside gleam
Primroses, orphans of the flowery prime.

Where is the girl who by the boatman's door,
    Above the locks, above the boating throng,
        Unmoored our skiff when through the Wytham flats,
    Red loosestrife and blond meadowsweet among,
        And darting swallows and light water gnats,
            We tracked the shy Thames shore?
Where are the mowers, who, as the tiny swell
    Of our boat passing heaved the river-grass,
    Stood with suspended scythe to see us pass?
They all are gone, and thou art gone as well!

Yes, thou art gone! and round me too the night
    In ever-nearing circle weaves her shade.
        I see her veil draw soft across the day,
    I feel her slowly chilling breath invade
        The cheek grown thin, the brown hair sprent with grey;
            I feel her finger light
Laid pausefully upon life's headlong train;
    The foot less prompt to meet the morning dew,
    The heart less bounding at emotion new,
And hope, once crushed, less quick to spring again.

And long the way appears, which seemed so short
　To the less-practised eye of sanguine youth;
　　And high the mountain tops, in cloudy air,
　The mountain tops where is the throne of Truth,
　　Tops in life's morning sun so bright and bare!
　　　Unbreachable the fort
　Of the long-battered world uplifts its wall;
　　And strange and vain the earthly turmoil grows,
　　And near and real the charm of thy repose,
And night as welcome as a friend would fall.

But hush! the upland hath a sudden loss
　Of quiet! Look, adown the dusk hill-side,
　　A troop of Oxford hunters going home,
　As in old days, jovial and talking, ride.
　　From hunting with the Berkshire hounds they come.
　　　Quick! let me fly, and cross
　Into yon farther field! – 'Tis done; and see,
　　Backed by the sunset, which doth glorify
　　The orange and pale violet evening sky,
Bare on its lonely ridge, the Tree! the Tree!

I take the omen! Eve lets down her veil,
　The white fog creeps from bush to bush about,
　　The west unflushes, the high stars grow bright,
　And in the scattered farms the lights come out.
　　I cannot reach the signal-tree tonight,
　　　Yet, happy omen, hail!
　Hear it from thy broad lucent Arno vale
　　(For there thine earth-forgetting eyelids keep
　　The morningless and unawakening sleep
　Under the flowery oleanders pale),

Hear it, O Thyrsis, still our tree is there!
    Ah, vain! These English fields, this upland dim,
        These brambles pale with mist engarlanded,
    That lone, sky-pointing tree, are not for him:
        To a boon southern country he is fled,
            And now in happier air,
    Wandering with the great Mother's train divine
        (And purer or more subtle soul than thee,
        I trow, the mighty Mother doth not see)
    Within a folding of the Apennine,

Thou hearest the immortal chants of old!
    Putting his sickle to the perilous grain
        In the hot cornfield of the Phrygian king,
    For thee the Lityerses song again
        Young Daphnis with his silver voice doth sing;
            Sings his Sicilian fold,
    His sheep, his hapless love, his blinded eyes –
        And how a call celestial round him rang,
        And heavenward from the fountain-brink he sprang,
    And all the marvel of the golden skies.

There thou art gone, and me thou leavest here
    Sole in these fields! yet will I not despair.
        Despair I will not, while I yet descry
    'Neath the mild canopy of English air
        That lonely tree against the western sky.
            Still, still these slopes, 'tis clear,
    Our Gipsy-Scholar haunts, outliving thee!
        Fields where soft sheep from cages pull the hay,
        Woods with anemones in flower till May,
    Know him a wanderer still; then why not me?

A fugitive and gracious light he seeks,
   Shy to illumine; and I seek it too.
      This does not come with houses or with gold,
   With place, with honour and a flattering crew;
         'Tis not in the world's market bought and sold;
            But the smooth-slipping weeks
   Drop by, and leave its seeker still untired;
      Out of the heed of mortals he is gone,
      He wends unfollowed, he must house alone;
   Yet on he fares, by his own heart inspired.

Thou too, O Thyrsis, on like quest wast bound!
   Thou wanderedst with me for a little hour!
      Men gave thee nothing; but this happy quest,
   If men esteemed thee feeble, gave thee power,
         If men procured thee trouble, gave thee rest.
            And this rude Cumner ground,
   Its fir-topped Hurst, its farms, its quiet fields,
      Here cam'st thou in thy jocund youthful time,
      Here was thine height of strength, thy golden prime!
   And still the haunt beloved a virtue yields.

What though the music of thy rustic flute
   Kept not for long its happy, country tone;
      Lost it too soon, and learnt a stormy note
   Of men contention-tost, of men who groan,
         Which tasked thy pipe too sore, and tired thy throat —
            It failed, and thou wast mute!
   Yet hadst thou alway visions of our light,
      And long with men of care thou couldst not stay,
      And soon thy foot resumed its wandering way,
   Left human haunt, and on alone till night.

Too rare, too rare, grow now my visits here!
>   'Mid city noise, not, as with thee of yore,
>>   Thyrsis! in reach of sheep bells is my home.
>   – Then through the great town's harsh, heart-wearying roar,
>>   Let in thy voice a whisper often come,
>>>   To chase fatigue and fear:
> *Why faintest thou? I wandered till I died.*
>>   *Roam on! The light we sought is shining still.*
>>   *Dost thou ask proof! Our tree yet crowns the hill,*
> *Our Scholar travels yet the loved hill-side.*

1862–65

Palladium

Set where the upper streams of Simois flow
Was the Palladium, high 'mid rock and wood;
And Hector was in Ilium, far below,
And fought, and saw it not – but there it stood!

It stood, and sun and moonshine rained their light
On the pure columns of its glen-built hall.
Backward and forward rolled the waves of fight
Round Troy; but while this stood, Troy could not fall.

So, in its lovely moonlight, lives the soul.
Mountains surround it, and sweet virgin air;
Cold plashing, past it, crystal waters roll:
We visit it by moments, ah, too rare!

Men will renew the battle in the plain
Tomorrow: red with blood will Xanthus be;
Hector and Ajax will be there again,
Helen will come upon the wall to see.

Then we shall rust in shade, or shine in strife,
And fluctuate 'twixt blind hopes and blind despairs,
And fancy that we put forth all our life,
And never know how with the soul it fares.

Still doth the soul, from its lone fastness high,
Upon our life a ruling effluence send;
And when it fails, fight as we will, we die;
And, while it lasts, we cannot wholly end.

(?) 1864

A Wish

I ask not that my bed of death
From bands of greedy heirs be free;
For these besiege the latest breath
Of fortune's favoured sons, not me.

I ask not each kind soul to keep
Tearless, when of my death he hears.
Let those who will, if any, weep!
There are worse plagues on Earth than tears.

I ask but that my death may find
The freedom to my life denied;
Ask but the folly of mankind
Then, then at last, to quit my side.

Spare me the whispering, crowded room,
The friends who come, and gape, and go;
The ceremonious air of gloom –
All which makes death a hideous show!

Nor bring, to see me cease to live,
Some doctor full of phrase and fame,
To shake his sapient head, and give
The ill he cannot cure a name.

Nor fetch, to take the accustomed toll
Of the poor sinner bound for death,

His brother-doctor of the soul,
To canvass with official breath

The future and its viewless things —
That undiscovered mystery
Which one who feels death's winnowing wings
Must needs read clearer, sure, than he!

Bring none of these; but let me be,
While all around in silence lies,
Moved to the window near, and see
Once more, before my dying eyes,

Bathed in the sacred dews of morn
The wide aërial landscape spread —
The world which was ere I was born,
The world which lasts when I am dead;

Which never was the friend of *one*,
Nor promised love it could not give,
But lit for all its generous sun,
And lived itself, and made us live.

There let me gaze, till I become
In soul, with what I gaze on, wed!
To feel the universe my home;
To have before my mind — instead

Of the sick room, the mortal strife,
The turmoil for a little breath —
The pure eternal course of life,
Not human combatings with death!

Thus feeling, gazing, might I grow
Composed, refreshed, ennobled, clear;
Then willing let my spirit go
To work or wait elsewhere or here!

(?) 1865

Growing Old

What is it to grow old?
Is it to lose the glory of the form,
The lustre of the eye?
Is it for beauty to forgo her wreath?
– Yes, but not this alone.

Is it to feel our strength –
Not our bloom only, but our strength – decay?
Is it to feel each limb
Grow stiffer, every function less exact,
Each nerve more loosely strung?

Yes, this, and more; but not,
Ah! 'tis not what in youth we dreamed 'twould be.
'Tis not to have our life
Mellowed and softened as with sunset glow,
A golden day's decline.

'Tis not to see the world
As from a height, with rapt prophetic eyes,
And heart profoundly stirred;
And weep, and feel the fullness of the past,
The years that are no more.

It is to spend long days,
And not once feel that we were ever young;
It is to add, immured
In the hot prison of the present, month
To month with weary pain.

It is to suffer this,
And feel but half, and feebly, what we feel.
Deep in our hidden heart
Festers the dull remembrance of a change,
But no emotion – none.

It is – last stage of all –
When we are frozen up within, and quite
The phantom of ourselves,
To hear the world applaud the hollow ghost,
Which blamed the living man.

1864–67

'Below the surface-stream'

Below the surface-stream, shallow and light,
Of what we *say* we feel – below the stream,
As light, of what we *think* we feel – there flows
With noiseless current strong, obscure and deep,
The central stream of what we feel indeed.

(?) 1869

The Last Word

Creep into thy narrow bed,
Creep, and let no more be said!
Vain thy onset! all stands fast.
Thou thyself must break at last.

Let the long contention cease!
Geese are swans, and swans are geese.
Let them have it how they will!
Thou art tired; best be still.

They out-talked thee, hissed thee, tore thee?
Better men fared thus before thee;
Fired their ringing shot, and passed,
Hotly charged – and sank at last.

Charge once more, then, and be dumb!
Let the victors, when they come,
When the forts of folly fall,
Find thy body by the wall!

1864–67

NOTE ON THE TEXT

My selection is chronological as far as it is possible to judge, generally based on the Allotts' superb 1979 edition (see over). Arnold was an incorrigible shuffler and tweaker, but the texts here (though not the particular arrangements within sequences) are taken from the 1885 collected edition, *Poems*, which Arnold himself oversaw. The date of composition is given beneath each poem.

I have discreetly modernised some of Arnold's punctuation (where there is a semicolon followed by a dash, for example) but have reluctantly left many of the innumerable exclamation marks and a good number of the hyphens (although I drew the line at *to-day*, *to-morrow* and *to-night*). Spelling is equally thorny, especially when it comes to 'Gipsy' or 'Gypsy'. The publisher and I discussed this at length and, although inclined to update it (since the sound would not be affected), we felt such a celebrated poem as 'The Scholar-Gipsy' should not be too much tampered with. We have, however, capitalised 'Gipsy' throughout; it is, after all, the word that has been frowned upon by the Roma, rather than its spelling. One or two archaisms I have silently modernised – notably 'sate', which jars in the otherwise quite plainspoken 'The Forsaken Merman', although I have left it in those poems with a loftier register or where it is needed for a rhyme. In most cases, I have followed earlier editors and retained Arnold's choices.

Inevitably, I have had to omit entire poems of significance ('Empedocles on Etna' really needs to be read in full), but there are several complete long poems and extracts from others.

JG

NOTES ON THE POEMS

The poet is referred to throughout as MA. 'The Allotts' are Kenneth and Miriam Allott, whose edition of the poems remains the fullest and most reliable.

27 'Mycerinus': The Egyptian story of Mycerinus, Cheops's son, comes from Herodotus. Having heard from an oracle that he had only six years to live, he was so resentful at this reward for his virtuous life (by comparison with his immoral father and uncle) that he resolved to make merry for the rest of his life. It was composed not long after Dr Arnold died prematurely and MA was warned that he may have inherited the same heart condition.

32 'A Question: To Fausta': The dedicatee is MA's sister, Jane (also known as 'K').

33 'Shakespeare': A sonnet, but not a Shakespearian one. In his forthright biography, A.L. Rowse calls the famous opening lines 'largely nonsense' and attributes the idea of Shakespeare's obscurity to MA's 'youthful ignorance'.

34 'In Utrumque Paratus': Readers troubled by the density and obscurity of this little-known poem may prefer to pass by its lofty artifice, but it does represent a certain facet of Arnold's work which he didn't develop. It is one example of what MA called in his Preface 'the dialogue of the mind with itself'. He had been reading Plotinus. John Fuller examines the poem in his book, *Who is Ozymandias?* He suggests (or MA's father might have suggested) the title could be translated as 'Ready for anywhere'. The motto was on the crest of his aunt's husband's family.

36 'Resignation: To Fausta': This is the middle section of a 275-line poem. In addressing his sister so nostalgically, MA is following the example of Wordsworth in 'Tintern Abbey'.

NOTES ON THE POEMS

Jane had been suffering depression following the broken engagement to George Cotton, a misfortune which some biographers have suggested may have precipitated their father's death.

42 'The Forsaken Merman': From a Danish ballad, 'Agnes and the Merman', encountered in Hans Christian Andersen or George Borrow. It owes something to the Goethe of 'The Sorcerer's Apprentice', and has a power which transcends any sentimentality. The shifting metres (the sudden 'Down, down, down!') are especially effective and give the poem a symphonic structure.

47 'To a Republican Friend, 1848': Written for 'Citizen Clough' (the title MA used when he sent a letter to his revolutionary friend and poetic rival). The Allotts speculate that 'Earth's great ones' are Thomas Carlyle, Ralph Waldo Emerson, George Sand.

49 'Switzerland': MA shuffled these poems for various editions, perhaps to cover his tracks. I have omitted 'A Memory-Picture' and placed separately at the end 'The Terrace at Berne', sometimes included as part of the Marguerite sequence, though composed long after he had married Flu. It was in Thun that MA originally met (or perhaps only saw) a girl with blue eyes, and all we really know of 'Marguerite' is what he mentions in letters. The Berne poem was written when he was a married man, and in fact the 'fair stranger' in 'Absence' must surely be Lucy, given the grey eyes. Nicholas Murray points out in his biography that MA told his daughters (as a 'smiling Victorian pater familias') Marguerite did not exist.

68 'Youth's Agitations': A Shakespearian sonnet, unlike most of MA's. This was part of a projected sequence of five.

65 'Stanzas in Memory of the Author of *Obermann*': This extract (lines 93–148) omits the poem's long-drawn-out conclusion and the opening tributes to Wordsworth and Goethe (other

poems here cover the same ground). Étienne Pivert de Senancour is largely forgotten now, but MA felt emotional kinship with the author's hero, unsure of his faith, tormented by wayward thoughts and desires.

69 'Empedocles on Etna': MA was in two minds about his book-length dramatic poem (almost a poetic drama), withdrawing it and later reprinting it. Empedocles is disillusioned with life and resolves to kill himself. His words are intermittently juxtaposed with the brighter pastoral tones of his disciple, young Callicles. The first extract here is one of Callicles' harp songs from the beginning of Act I, Scene 2. The second is from Empedocles final soliloquy at the end of Act II: having accepted that everything returns 'to the elements it came from' he asks himself what becomes of the mind. Shortly after, he plunges into the cone of Etna.

73 'Tristram and Iseult': The story tells how a love potion made Tristram fall in love with Queen Iseult of Ireland, but he was obliged to marry a different Iseult (in Brittany). This mere taster (MA's long narrative is one of his most formally inventive) comes from Book III, whose focus is the faithful 'Iseult of the White Hands' after her husband's death. Nicholas Murray points out that this was 'the first modern treatment' of the legend; Richard Wagner's opera *Tristan und Isolde* came thirteen years later. When MA saw the opera in Munich, he felt he had 'managed the story better than Wagner'.

75 'Faded Leaves': These poems about the relationship with MA's future wife were grouped together in 1855. Perhaps because they were too revealing, only the last five stanzas of 'The River' were originally published, and this longer version is much less well known.

81 'Memorial Verses': The Arnolds were good friends with Wordsworth and his associates. That MA commemorates him by way of Goethe and Byron reflects their parallel

importance to him. The River Rotha (or Rothay) flows near Grasmere churchyard.

84 'The Youth of Nature': This contemplation of Wordsworth is what MA called a 'pindaric' – unrhymed verse, generally with three stresses to a line. It is a less dramatic version of what Hopkins would do with his sprung rhythm.

89 'Dover Beach': See comments in the introduction. That the poem was in MA's mind during his honeymoon seems incontrovertible, making the line break between 'true' and 'To one another' especially potent. The poet's depth of confused feeling for the addressee is equalled by the depth of his concern about the embattled world they inhabit. The simile in the last three lines alludes to Thucydides' description of a night battle, a passage well known at the time – especially as applied by John Newman to the Tractarian controversies. For MA's final collected edition, he substituted 'land' for 'sand' in the eighth line. Dover remained one of his favourite places in England.

91 'The Buried Life': This poem owes much to the Stoics' belief that there is a deep hidden self, but MA had also been reading the *Bhagavad Gita*. He was preoccupied with the way our apparent freedom is mysteriously predestined.

95 'Lines Written in Kensington Gardens': The influence of both Wordsworth and Goethe can be seen in this poem.

97 'The Future': A tricky subject to bring off (only Les Murray has managed it as successfully); probably written around the time MA was engaged to Lucy Wightman. 'He wots of' means 'He knows of'. The unusual choice of 'shot' in line 57 is correct: think of quivering shot silk.

101 'A Summer Night': The Allotts suggest that the opening lines may refer to May 1851 after MA's engagement when he 'went several times late at night to gaze at [Lucy's] window in her father's house', and the most likely setting for the remembered night is Calais.

- *105* 'Stanzas from the Grande Chartreuse': The Carthusians enforce silence. A 'sciolist' is someone who has strong opinions on something of which they know little. The theological clashes of the Oxford Movement and his father's involvement echo in this poem. MA's line in the eighth stanza before the end originally read 'We praise them, but they are not ours'. See JG's own stanzas in the appendix.
- *113* 'Sohrab and Rustum': MA's most Homeric (or Miltonic) poem, and perhaps (consciously or not) the one that confronts his own father most powerfully. It is best not to let all the lists and epic similes and obscure names – some of which, such as 'Ader-baijan', are familiar in different spellings – hold up the flow of the narrative, which is clear enough and maintains the tension. There are various moments when the narrative could go either way. It can almost be enjoyed like a feature film, allowing the background music and spectacularly vivid detail (not to mention those sentimental moments with a faithful steed) to sweep us on.
- *142* 'The Scholar-Gipsy': If 'Sohrab and Rustum' is a homage to Milton, here the inspiration seems to be Keats (a poet he didn't usually like). The elaborate form is a variation of 'Ode to a Nightingale'. The story comes from a seventeenth-century book by Joseph Glanvill, and it had a private significance for MA and Clough while at Oxford. The Allotts describe the Scholar-Gipsy as 'a Callicles miraculously preserved from turning into an Empedocles'. The 'pink convolvulus' of the third stanza were blue in an earlier version. A 'lasher' (tenth stanza) is the pool below a weir. That controversial critic Geoffrey Grigson was much struck by this word and claimed (shrewdly) he could only enjoy a few lines in MA 'occasioned by orchids, fritillaries, cuckoos, lashers and storms, in which Arnold preserves the accessible to all of us, in a peculiar felicity, without frill or lag.'

NOTES ON THE POEMS

151 'Requiescat': No commentator seems clear quite when or about whom this was written. It has been suggested MA was imagining Marguerite's death, much as Wordsworth imagined his Lucy's; but of course Marguerite herself may be imaginary.

152 'Balder Dead': The poem draws on the stories in the Old Norse *Prose Edda*. I have selected the description of Valhalla at the opening of Book II from this 565-line blank-verse narrative about the Norse god, Balder, in which Ragnarok, the end of the world, is anticipated. It is perhaps unfortunate that MA refers to the Fates as Nornies rather than Norns; but other names sound familiar – the so-called All-Father, Odin, his feasting hall, Valhalla, where Valkyries bring dead warriors, Bifrost, the rainbow bridge guarded by Heimdall, and Midgard, the world of humans.

153 'Haworth Churchyard, April 1855': Prompted by Charlotte Brontë's death and what MA thought would be Harriet Martineau's. In fact, she lived a further two decades, and publication was consequently delayed. Also, he discovered (from Elizabeth Gaskell) that Anne was buried in Scarborough, while Charlotte, Emily and Bramwell are in Haworth church vault, so no 'grass/Blows'. The poem is bold metrically: mainly three stresses to a line, but with exceptions, and varied numbers of syllables. It is best not to dwell on MA's uncharacteristically dismissive remark about the 'rough, grimed race'.

158 'Rugby Chapel': MA's powerful extended metaphor draws on his father's love of hiking and climbing. The sincerity of feeling just manages to carry the poem through its emphatically heroic finale, which is rather heavy on the brass. A.L. Rowse remarked sourly of this 'perhaps too famous tribute' that 'the metre is unrhymed and uncongenial, and, though there is unstinted admiration, there is no love in it.'

- *166* 'Stanzas from Carnac': While visiting schools in France, MA received news that his brother Willy had died. Written the following month after a visit to the Neolithic standing stones, this poem has (as his biographer Park Honan puts it) a 'bland, sunlit emptiness'.
- *168* 'Rachel': Rachel Félix (usually just known as Rachel) was a French tragic actor who died young in 1858. MA had seen her on stage ten times, acting in plays by Racine and Corneille.
- *170* 'West London': Lyric poets are inclined to fall back on the sonnet as they get older, but Robert Browning encouraged MA to print this (and one about east London not included here). It is something of a riposte to Wordsworth's 'Earth hath not anything to show more fair'.
- *171* 'Worldly Place': MA had been reading the *Meditations* of Stoic philosopher-emperor Marcus Aurelius. The drudgery of his 'charming occupation' as a school inspector seems to be weighing on him.
- *172* 'Thyrsis': In classical convention, poets are 'piping' shepherds (Thyrsis appears in Virgil). This tribute to a fellow 'swain', a shrewd and touching sequel to 'The Scholar-Gipsy', is also an elegy for what MA felt were his own waning poetic powers ('My pipe is lost'). It includes, ironically, one of his most enduring phrases – 'dreaming spires', coined to describe Oxford.
- *181* 'Palladium': The Palladium was a wooden statue of Pallas Athene, protector of Troy. The critic Douglas Bush says of this poem that it is 'as simply didactic as a pulpit anecdote but one of Arnold's best'.
- *182* 'A Wish': In a letter to his mother, MA expresses distaste for the 'ceremonial' of death and says he would like to die 'in a place like Rome, and be buried in peace' with perhaps just one acquaintance present.

- *185* 'Growing Old': A response to Browning's breezily cheery view of ageing in 'Rabbi Ben Ezra' ('the best is yet to be'). It anticipates the Eliot of 'Little Gidding' (on 'the gifts reserved for age') and Larkin's 'The Old Fools'.
- *187* 'Below the surface stream': The image of the underground river is a favourite of MA's.
- *188* 'The Last Word': MA's lifelong exasperation with Philistines comes to the surface here. One wonders what he would have made of our own hissing online world in which 'Geese are swans, and swans are geese'.

Recommended Reading

ARNOLD'S POETRY AND PROSE:
The Poems of Matthew Arnold, ed. Kenneth Allott/2nd edition ed. Miriam Allott (London: Longman, 1965, revised 1979)

Culture and Anarchy and Other Selected Prose, ed. P.J. Keating (London: Penguin, 1970, reissued 2015)

Matthew Arnold: Selected Writings, ed. Seamus Perry (Oxford: OUP, 2020)

BIOGRAPHIES:
A.L. Rowse, *Matthew Arnold: Poet and Prophet* (London: Thames and Hudson, 1976)

Park Honan, *Matthew Arnold: A Life* (London: Weidenfeld & Nicholson, 1981)

Ian Hamilton, *A Gift Imprisoned: The Poetic Life of Matthew Arnold* (London: Bloomsbury, 1998)

Nicholas Murray, *A Life of Matthew Arnold* (London: Hodder & Stoughton, 1999)

OTHER WRITINGS ON ARNOLD:
T.S. Eliot, *The Use of Poetry and the Use of Criticism* (London: Faber and Faber, 1933)

Douglas Bush, *Matthew Arnold* (London: Macmillan, 1971)

Tony Roberts, *A Movement of Mind: Essays on Poets, Critics & Biographers* (Nottingham: Shoestring Press, 2024)

Acknowledgments

Thanks to Baylor University Press and my editor, Kevin Gardner, for allowing the reprint of my poem, originally titled, 'Stanzas from the Grande Chartreuse', from *The Interpretation of Owls: Selected Poems 1977–2022*. Certain passages in the introduction appeared in an essay commissioned by *Poetry London*, 'Wandering Between Two Worlds', for which my thanks to the editor, Niall Campbell. Thanks also to Daljit Nagra, Penelope Shuttle and Alicia Stallings. As always, I am grateful to Will Dady of Renard Press for embracing this project.

INDEX OF TITLES

A Question, 32
A Summer Night, 101
A Wish, 182
Balder Dead, 152
'Below the surface-stream', 187
Dover Beach, 89
Empedocles on Etna, 69
Faded Leaves, 75
Growing Old, 185
Haworth Churchyard, 153
In Utrumque Paratus, 34
Lines Written in Kensington
    Gardens, 95
Memorial Verses, 81
Mycerinus, 27
Palladium, 181
Quiet Work, 48
Rachel, 168
Requiescat, 151
Resignation, 36
Rugby Chapel, 158
Shakespeare, 33
Sohrab and Rustum, 113
Stanzas from Carnac, 166
Stanzas from the Grande
    Chartreuse, 105
Stanzas in Memory of the Author
    of *Obermann*, 65

Switzerland, 49
The Buried Life, 91
The Forsaken Merman, 42
The Future, 97
The Last Word, 188
The Scholar-Gipsy, 142
The Terrace at Berne, 62
The Youth of Nature, 84
Thyrsis, 172
To a Republican Friend, 1848, 47
Tristram and Iseult, 73
West London, 170
Worldly Place, 171
Youth's Agitations, 68

APPENDIX

Two Poems by John Greening

Further Stanzas from the Grande Chartreuse

They set off through the bitter cold, and he
is full of what a night it was – the cells,
the silence, candlelight and pax – while she
is longing for some warmth. There are no mules
and he's decided they can walk: the mist
has gone so Matt, of course, cannot resist

the lure of Alpine peaks. His pristine wife
takes some convincing, having spent the night
apart while he inspected man's belief
in what he can't believe. She'd sensed her fate
last night as they approached: the chill, the roar
below from an unseen river, Guiers Mort.

At least this morning he has deigned to speak,
is even cheerful (*Excelsior!*) as they climb
his choice of narrow, slippery mountain track
for three hours, till she asks about the time
and where they are. The high Alps glisten.
He starts to talk, and she can only listen.

By chance, they find a chalet, where he hires
a mule and then insists they carry on
to Les Chapieux. A local guide declares
it isn't wise, but Matthew Arnold's done
with teachers – Nature (as Wordsworth said) is school.
So Fanny Lucy climbs on to the mule.

Without a saddle, perched there, she is led –
her poet-husband trailing far behind –
towards a maze of ice (if she had stayed
in Hampton!) along a razor's edge, no ground
in sight, a snowy chasm stretching out
beneath her, epic similes of doubt.

It is as if he's somehow conjured this
from his own mind's cold sophistries, a vent
of bubbling myth. As though Empedocles
were holding that long rein way out in front
and leading her beside a seething cone,
where sparks of warmth mean poetry alone.

> From *The Interpretation of Owls: Selected Poems 1977–2022*,
> ed. Kevin Gardner (Texas: Baylor University Press, 2023)

A Walk with Matthew Arnold

A quiet evening in Liverpool, and he
suggests a walk, having already noticed
that little fence (just two feet, nine inches high)
dividing the garden from the estuary.

At school, he once leapt over a gate almost
as tall as him, though he'd not told his father,
and felt like an earthy football converting
itself between rigid posts after a try.

At Oxford, he bet five pounds that he could jump
from Wadham's soft lawns up across its high, spiked
railings on to the hard reality of
a pavement. Those first anarchical essays.

Suddenly, all nineteen stone of the poet,
critic and internationally known man
of letters turns to smile at his friend, then starts
to run, forgetting perhaps the angina

and the sixty-five years, three months he carries
as he leaps, indeed lands, quite safely on the
banks of the Mersey and another Sunday.
But his heart is racing. A ship draws nearer

bringing his daughter home. He will sit through church,
then lunch, half a brandy, and walk with his wife
towards the tram stop, pausing once, twice, and now
hurrying as the horses wait, and he falls.

ABOUT JOHN GREENING

John Greening is a Bridport, Arvon and Cholmondeley winner, author of *From the East* (Renard Press, 2024) and more than two dozen other poetry collections, notably *The Interpretation of Owls: Selected Poems 1977–2022* (Baylor University Press, ed. Kevin Gardner). He has edited Edmund Blunden, Geoffrey Grigson, Iain Crichton Smith and most recently U.A. Fanthorpe. As well as several critical studies and translations (of Goethe), there have been anthologies such as *Contraflow: Lines of Englishness* co-edited with Kevin Gardner. A book of linked essays, photographs and poems, *A High Calling*, appears from Renard in 2025 when his versions of Rilke's complete *New Poems* are also due from Baylor.

A NOTE ON SUSTAINABILITY

RENARD PRESS feels strongly that there is no denying the climate crisis, and we all have a part to play in fixing the problem.

We are proud to be one of the UK's first climate-positive publishers, taking more carbon out of the air than we put in. How? We reduce our emissions as much as possible, using green energy, printing locally and choosing the materials we use carefully; we calculate our carbon footprint and doubly offset it through gold-standard schemes; we replant the trees used to make our books and we plant a tree for every order we receive via our website.

Find out more at:
RENARDPRESS.COM/ECO